TAKE CARE

tales, tips and love from women caregivers

Edited by Elayne Clift

D1453048

Acknowledgments

Special acknowledgment goes to my friend Eileen Higgins, who brought this idea to me and allowed me to run with it. I am also indebted to all the women who took the time and care to respond to my call for contributions, including those whose work does not appear in the book. I am also grateful to David Braughler and Craig Ramsdell at Braughler Books with whom it is always a pleasure to collaborate.

Dedication

To the multitude of women caregivers who I know and respect, and to those I don't know ~ all of whom I humbly include in my list of heroes and role models.

Photo of hearts and hands: iStock.com/brozova

Printed in the United States of America

First Printing, 2017

ISBN 978-1-945091-13-1

Ordering Information: Special discounts are available on quantity
purchases by bookstores, corporations, associations, and others. For
details, contact the publisher at:

    sales@braughlerbooks.com
    or at 937-58-BOOKS

For questions or comments about this book, please write to:

    info@braughlerbooks.com

**Braughler
Books**
braughlerbooks.com

Contents

Preface

Women have always been caregivers. Whether looking after small children, elders, other family members or friends in small communities, tending to others in urban settings with limited support systems, or acting as professional caregivers in institutional settings, we have been the primary providers of physical care and emotional support in a variety of settings and circumstances throughout the ages.

Today that remains true, and being the main caregiver may be more vital to understand than ever. As women have children later and elders live longer, we are challenged by competing demands and shrinking resources. Many of us have elderly parents living (perhaps with us) in a time of growing dementia or increasing frailty; others have parents who need supervision in nursing homes of dubious quality. At the same time, we are parenting children who quite often have their own physical or emotional challenges. We may also have spouses in failing health who need our attention. And who among us would not be there for an ill friend or family member?

Whether we are younger women focused on caring for our children, older women charged with "being there" for a sick spouse or parent, or women in-between those two stages of life who are called upon to take care of others, many of us find ourselves in the caregiver role, well before we expected to be there and often feeling less prepared than we wish. This book is for them.

My own experience with caregiving began at an early age. My parents had married late, and while my two siblings and I were still young, both our father and mother suffered from chronic and often debilitating conditions: asthma and depression respectively. By the time I was in high school and my older sister had married, I had taken on many of the demanding tasks of caregiving, including carrying out the responsibilities that keep a home going and taking care of (and worrying about) my younger brother. After our father's death, looking out for my mother's best interests and ensuring her care became paramount tasks that went on for many years until she died at the age of 86.

During those years when my husband's work demanded that I be "wife of," I had a job of my own that I loved, and we had two children. As if that weren't enough, I was also completing a graduate degree and doing important volunteer work with "underprivileged" women, all of which is to say that my caretaking role was diverse and difficult.

So I understood early on what it means to be a caretaker, and that's why doing this anthology was so important to me, especially in a time when more and more will be asked of us, given changing demographics in an increasingly challenging world. I hope this book will let women caregivers know that they are not alone, that they can survive what they have committed to on behalf of people they love, and that the tasks they have assumed, and the love with which they embrace those tasks, is not only appreciated but deeply respected, even if we are so fortunate as never to need similar help and dedication.

Elayne Clift, April, 2017

All the Longing Left in the Body[1]

An Introduction by Kate Gray

It could be you stopping me, the fluorescent bulbs harsh in the women's restroom after the dingy light of the highway for more than a hundred miles, the sun barely rising behind all those clouds over the Columbia River. It could be you, maybe not the you sitting here reading, but the you quite a few years from now, speaking with a rough voice, half of your face a little lower than the other, your hair turned gray and your clothes neatly tucked. On I-84, eastbound, after climbing out of the Columbia River Gorge and onto the grasslands near Umatilla, after pulling off the road at Boardman, Oregon, in the wind and wet, you would probably do the same thing that she did in the women's restroom, if you were in her shoes.

"Sorry," she said as she passed me in the entrance to the women's room. "That's my husband in the other stall. Don't mind him." She was going back to her car.

Her husband was in the farthest stall, the one typically large enough for a wheelchair to turn around. There was one stall left for me. Driving since 5:15 AM from Portland, I was racing east to Pendleton for a conference, not sure how long the drive would be or what the weather in late October might present. Through the Gorge and on to the prairie, the roads could produce wind gusts that blew you into the next lane or ice that tossed you

---

[1] First appeared in *The Rumpus Blog*, July 2013. Reprinted by permission of the author.

into basalt cliffs or sagebrush. The day before, the highway was closed due to ice and accidents. That day, the balmy winds blew gray and soggy. I was ready for a stop.

Behind the blue metal door, with the latch that left just enough gap to make me watch the door, I heard nothing from the husband next to me, and I thought about older men taking a long time in the bathroom, how my oldest brother rolls his eyes now when he emerges from a long stint. Nothing about an older man in the stall next to me made me nervous. This restroom, with cement-block walls and a cement floor, had one of those round communal sinks, like ones in elementary schools, but this one was motion-activated. Hot water and a functioning soap dispenser made me think that federal funds for highway improvements had reached out here in the last few years for retrofitting. Pleased with the mirror, which wasn't too scratched, though it did show how tired I looked, I left the silent man in the other stall and headed back to the car.

There were only two cars parked by this restroom: mine and the older woman's, a sturdy car like a Bonneville, gray as the sky. She was rounding the driver's side to return to the restroom when she looked up at me.

"Thank you," she said, "for understanding." In her right hand were her keys, and in her left was a blue, waffled diaper, disposable, a lighter kind than the ones I had helped my sister pull up recently when she was finished using the restroom.

"Everything okay?" I said.

The woman paused, breathed a little, raised her eyes with a slight smile on half her face. "Fine," she said. "Thank you." And she made her way up the path to the women's restroom and her husband in the large stall.

Without warning one Friday last March, my sister came in from pruning roses complaining of a fierce headache. My brother-in-law asked her to say his name, and when she said his name, "John," as if the word were taffy pulled in her mouth, he called an ambulance, and in seven minutes, the paramedics called a helicopter, and in an hour, she was in one of the best ICUs in the world. No one expected her to recover as quickly as she did from the massive brain bleed. She learned to walk after six weeks, feed herself after seven, move from the bed to the bathroom in eight.

What galled my sister, Kim, the most about the sudden disability was that she couldn't go to the bathroom in appropriate places at appropriate times. Eating pureed hamburgers and pureed pancakes and pureed apple pie a la mode was nothing compared to her discomfort when she wet the bed. She apologized profusely to the aides. Soon she learned the warning signs and asked for help. Her husband learned how to bend with his knees, lower himself to hug her, wrap his arms around her ribcage, and lift her off the bed to her feet. When she was steady on both feet, she rested her forearms on his forearms, and they did a tight dance to turn her toward the walker and the direction she needed to move. He learned how to walk behind her when she shuffled into the wide expanse of the bathroom in the rehab facility. From aides and therapists, he learned how to lower her clothes to her ankles and lower her on to the toilet seat, then step outside.

Whenever I waited outside the bathroom door with him, and heard the flush, he would wink at me, say, "That's my cue," and he would lean toward the door, his hand resting on the handle, say to Kim, "Darling, is it time?" And he learned how to wipe her clean, how to put the blue diaper between her legs and tape the sides around her waist, how to pull up her pants around her diaper and leave her shirt untucked, just the way she liked it.

When my brother-in-law was out of the room one time, my sister said, "No one wants their husband to change their diaper." The process was hard on both of them, although they met the necessity with equal parts charm and grit.

It could be any of us, waiting outside a bathroom stall, coming up with the code or cue for "Come in" and the polite response, overcoming the body's instinct to grimace at the acrid smells, taking a diaper much bigger than the one used for an infant and folding it carefully, carrying it carefully, disposing of it. It could be any of us, bending down to hug our spouse or partner, wrap our arms under their arms, straighten our legs to lift the two of us to standing.

My partner and I have talked about dying but not about disability. We've talked about how one of us will die before the other and how the one left behind will have it worse than the one who dies. The one left behind has all the cleaning up to do, all the memories and reminders, all the longing left in the body. The one who dies just goes. The one left stays and lives without the ritual responses, without the spark of seeing the other at the door.

Death and disability are messy, like toddlers with their toys. They leave memories and abilities in unfindable places, strewn every which way. A long disability before death shifts everything. If I were the one needing help to pee, if I had to watch my partner clean me, change my diaper, overcome the body's revulsion when I know how sensitive she is to smell, if I knew how much my partner, Cheryl, were giving up each day to attend to my bowels and medications and mental state, I would be mortified and frustrated and angry. And if I knew I could do nothing, Cheryl would grow thinner and more tired, her smile flatter and her hair grayer, I would experience a type of torture, something like the way a tree leans on barbed wire, the pressure making the body take in the barbed wire eventually, growing around it, adapting to the inevitable. This slow, painful process seems worse than dying.

But the woman at the rest area did not look sad. She was matter-of-fact. She moved with purpose from the restroom to the car and back. She was as steadfast as those basalt cliffs in the gorge.

It could be you taking a trip. It could be you moving through the steps of getting your loved one from the car to the restroom and back to the car. It could be you loving someone so much that you take him into the women's room with you, that you find a way to make a dance out of changing a diaper, that you don't mind doing what you have to do, as long as you are two together.

PART ONE

Our
Mothers

Matriarchal Hot Potato

Margaret Elysia Garcia

As the emergency room staff readied my mother to be airlifted to UC San Francisco Medical Center, she turned to me on her stretcher and said, "I guess you didn't turn out to be too bad a daughter. But I'm disappointed in you for quitting your job. Think of all the brown kids you're letting them down who needed to see one of their own as a college professor. Oh and if I make it out of here alive I want a chocolate cake with chocolate frosting. Don't skimp."

"I love you too, mommy," I cried out assuming that all the ordering and condemning my life choices meant she loved me. We didn't know the details yet, but my mother had fallen down a flight of stairs and hit her head; clots formed and swelled. My mother - the one who is never weak--literally the brains of our family--the one who has walked through the fires of death and destruction and goes to bat for us was the one on the stretcher. Her hands covered her pounding head. My mother: The Virgo in charge of everything in its proper order, detailing our cars and reminding us when we needed them serviced. The one whose garage looks like it was set up for a nuclear apocalypse that my daughter affectionately named 'mini-Costco' could no longer be the matriarch. She was abdicating before my eyes.

I thought I had at least twenty years till I reached this point, and like most Californian Gen-Xers I know, I admit to a certain amount of arrested development. As '70s kids, we grew up too fast and then decided to catch up to childhood somewhere in the middle there. I had a husband, two kids, two careers, two cats, and now my two mothers to contend with. My mother's partner is nine years older than she and has needed a caregiver, and. my mother had recently let go the various not-quite-adequate caretakers and decided to take on the job herself.

I called my brother. "Get out here," I said, "Mom is critically hurt." He made arrangements to fly across the continent. Then I called my stepsister: "Get up here and take care of your mom while I tend to mine!" She made plans to drive up and stay with her mother. "Wow," I thought, "maybe I can do this matriarch-in-charge thing."

Then I called Mom 2 (as I call her). She can no longer drive, is easily confused, has trouble walking and has early dementia. Now she was scared. My mother had been on the verge of retiring to take care of Mom 2 full-time when the accident happened.

What happens when the caretaker suddenly needs care? What happens when the daughter who's been told all her life that she isn't cut out to take care of things suddenly has to do just that?

I told Mom 2 about the airlift. She cried and reprimanded me for not letting her speak to Mom before the decision was made, failing to understand that we were in life-or-death mode; we didn't have the luxury of time.

"UCSF has brain specialists. People from all over the west go there for care. You want the best people working on her—for her," I said.

"But I can't visit her, even though we're married. What if they treat me like I'm a just a friend? What if they don't put our calls through, because they're homophobic?!"

"They didn't airlift her to Alabama!" I said. "They airlifted her to San Francisco, for Heaven sake! Her brain is hurting. Talking on the phone isn't going to be an option."

She cried some more, and I felt like the worst person in the world, a total bust as the newly appointed matriarch.

That I wasn't cut out to be a caregiver is not really surprising. When we were sick as kids, my mother would hand us a bowl to throw up in, a cup of water to drink, and a baby Tylenol. "Only wake me if you see blood," she'd say.

Over the next forty-eight hours, I called my mother's two workplaces, stocked up on groceries, and ran essential errands. I also read about medical power of attorney. That's when panic set in. What if I had to figure out Mom's bills, taxes, and car maintenance schedules? What if my duties expanded to cooking, cleaning, and taking my two moms to appointments? What if I had to be kind and gentle while moving them along their path in a way that other people learn via family tradition?

Suddenly I longed to dance wildly while drinking martinis far, far away. I didn't want to be anyone's responsible, mature daughter. Nope. Uh-uh.

On the third day of my reign as matriarch, I fetched my daughter from school looking decidedly haggard and over-whelmed. I searched for emergency chocolate in my purse as my daughter sensed my angst from the passenger seat. Leaning into the passenger side door, she tapped my arm and handed me an organic chocolate bar. "Mom," she said, "You aren't the next matriarch. You're just the interim. I'm the next one."

I looked at my cocky ten-year old with a raised eyebrow.

"Grandma has been giving me lessons. She's taught me to do everything—money, investing, changing filters; I know where everything is kept including where the safe deposit key is. I can do everything, Mom, and I know when to do it and how to do it. This isn't your thing. Grandma and I are better at this."

At first I was incredulous, then indignant. Wasn't I the nat-ural successor? Had I missed the fact that the matriarch gene bypassed me and emerged in my progeny?

Once my mother felt better, she confessed that indeed, she'd been consciously giving Paloma lessons in matriarchy. "You're too much of an artist," she said. "It's just not who you are." She paused. "You're a good cook, though," she offered as consolation.

I had to admit that before her fall, I hadn't thought much about my two mothers' futures or the fact that I am their nearest living relative. I'd always assumed my mother would take care of Mom 2. Eventually, perhaps, we'd rent a place with a mother-in-law unit attached. It never occurred to me – or to her - that such a brilliant, strong woman might come to need help one day.

My mother did recover from her fall, and for the most part she's still the authority in our extended households. My daughter continues happily in matriarch training, hands poised to catch the matriarchal hot potato. I'm happy to have touched it once and then passed it on.

Sometimes, I realize now, a matriarchal wannabe's strength comes from knowing that someone else might be better suited to the job. And that's okay, because it's really about the one who needs care, and not so much about the one who gives it.

Yo-Yo Wisdom

Mary Wheeler

When I arrived in California to take care of my mother after her stroke, I had no idea that everything I needed to know was mastered from four childhood yo-yo concepts:

1. They go up and down.
2. You just have to hang on.
3. Expect them to get wound up.
4. Two tricks are easy to learn: walk the doggie and rock the baby.

Though I had read many books about stroke victims, I didn't know what to expect when I saw her. She had always been a steadfast mom. If our lives had been a baseball game, 2039 Edgewood Drive was home base. It was that safe place to land, whether I hit a home run, foul ball, or made an egregious error in the field of life. Whatever condition I was in, it felt safe pulling into the familiar driveway. After a toot-toot of my horn, Mom was there to greet me with her blue twinkling eyes, an apron tied around her waist, and fresh-baked oatmeal raisin cookies piled high in her vintage metal cake box tin.

On my visit she was there, but not fully. Hollow, shallow eyes searched mine, weak fingers clutched mine, and skin sagging on her bones resembling tissue paper with pockets of blackened spots on her arms made her hard to look at. It was a grand, yet strange evening of two sisters and Mom, a brief, emotional reunion. I had come to town to relieve my older sister, who'd spent a month with Mom since her release from the hospital. Elizabeth needed to go home, and I had the summer off, so it was my turn to help Mom adjust to what would be a post-stroke lifestyle.

The first thing Mom wanted to do was give me a tour of the house. "Things are different around here, Mary," she said stifling a rebellious grunt. "I'm supposed to be happy about this, but I'm not." She was pointing to the new handrail going upstairs and insisting she didn't need it. I cringed when we reached the bathroom. Mounted on the wall by the claw foot bathtub was a sturdy gripping bar and a plastic potty chair perched above the toilet.

That evening, holding hands, we walked cautiously down the block, careful to avoid the places where tree roots pushed the sidewalk up. Our conversation was atypically curtailed. I was conscious of her paying attention to stay balanced, so I followed her silent lead rather than fill the air with chatter. It was instantly clear to me: My visit would be about me being there for her no matter what she might need at any particular moment. So I gently reminded her to "stand up straight, relax your shoulders...." and remembered to encourage her with comments like "That's right, good job!" Sometimes her breathing became fast and anxious, and I reminded her to inhale slowly, hold the breath, and then exhale. When she tilted left, I helped her re-center. We hummed songs. We stopped to admire flowers. We listened to birds and watched the sunset. Yo-yo wisdom had kicked in.

After dinner, we began her slow bedtime routine, beginning with a bath in which she lathered up with Dove soap. I turned on classical music, and, familiar products in hand, Mom brushed her teeth and reached for mint-flavored floss. She slathered her body with Jergens lotion and sprinkled herself with baby powder. I quickly learned the importance of going slowly so that she could do everything in the order her brain remembered it. Familiarity was key to her routine.

I watched mom hoist herself into bed, grunting with pleasure as she arranged the blanket and pillow just the way she liked them. "I love sleeping, Mary; that's all I want to do is sleep. It's the high point of my day. I wish I could sleep forever." My eyes fought a flood of tears as the knot of grief gripped my throat. I mustered a prayer, sang her a song, and kissed her forehead. "Good night Mom. I love you. Call if you need me. Sleep tight."

Wow. What was I in for? Could I do this all summer? Uncomfortable thoughts tumbled in my head like tennis shoes in a dryer. Will she pass away while I'm here? Feeling scared, lonely and ill-equipped, I realized my pre-stroke mom had morphed into a ninety-five year old woman with serious needs, and I was in charge of her comfort and safety. The lessons of the yo-yo were real. We had walked the doggie and I had rocked her to sleep. It was time to stay calm, and not over-react.

I crawled into my childhood bed and scanned the room, my eyes taking in the familiar black and white photographs on the wall. In one picture Mom is a 1930s bride. In another I am in the first grade; I am missing two front teeth, and I am sitting on her lap. How could the all-American woman in this picture be the same frail woman now snoring across the hall?

For decades, Mom had been an amazing Californian who at age 95 taught water aerobics at the Y, volunteered at the library, sang in the choir, visited shut-ins, and played bridge on Friday nights. She had been a Hospice volunteer who helped her blind friend write Christmas cards. She ran the church Newcomer's Club and hosted a daily dog party in her backyard at 5:00 p.m. Everywhere I went, I heard, "Your mom is amazing!"

But her stroke had changed everything. Her right arm had become limp, making simple tasks challenging. In physical therapy she learned again how to open cans and shuffle cards. Three times a week we went to rehab for an hour each of physical, speech, and occupational therapy. I bit my tongue as I watched her struggle to draw or to recall facts from a short story she'd just heard or to practice walking stairs. It was painful to realize that she no longer knew the difference between a nickel and a quarter and that she couldn't write a check.

Her come-back was hard in so many ways, and it took incredible concentration. But slowly, slowly, Mom regained her strength and balance. Once again, she appeared to be amazing. But though she was making progress, Mom needed help. I witnessed burners left on, pants put on backwards, and hoses running for hours. It became clear that if Mom were to stay in her home, we would need to hire a caretaker.

Mom's front porch has a swing where we rocked every afternoon, looking through photo albums, reliving happier times. The swing had always been the place for meaningful conversations, so I chose it to broach the subject of having someone move in with her when I needed to leave. "No way! I don't need anyone!" She said adamantly. I reminded her how many times she had said, "When my time comes, keep me in this home. Don't ever put me in one of those facilities. I want to stay right here and have someone move in with me."

"This is for my peace of mind," I told her. "You can stay in your home this way and enjoy all of your routines. We will find the very best person to drive you where you need to go and to help you manage around here." Mom slowly softened to the idea.

The interviews began with two words guiding our desires for mom: security and autonomy. We wanted her safe, and we wanted her to maintain a sense of independence.

The plan was to hire someone from a health care agency who could come at 7:00 a.m. to help Mom get to the YMCA for her water aerobics class. That person would then take her on errands and see her through lunch. Mom could have the afternoon alone to read, putter, and rest. The caregiver would return at 5:00 p.m. to help prepare dinner and see Mom through to bedtime.

It felt surreal, hiring a perfect stranger to move in. Olga was our first candidate. She made a nice first impression, as she talked about love and devotion and tending her father when he was ill. Mom remained disengaged until Olga informed us her favorite pastime was watching daytime television. We hastened the tour and told Olga, "We'll get back with you." Later that afternoon Maria arrived. She was a chatty young mother in jeans. When asked to tell us about herself, she told us about road trips to casinos. Maria did not get a second interview either. Then Mary Elizabeth showed up. She wore her nametag on hospital scrubs and looked like the much-loved image of Aunt Jemima. When asked to tell us about herself, she said the church was her family. Mary Elizabeth made the cut after getting the indoor and backyard tour. She was a strong woman of faith with a hearty laugh who liked to make apple pies. We hired her.

She proved to be our Mary Poppins. Strong, wise, and experienced, Mary Elizabeth was a master of companionable silence. Familiar with geriatric stroke patients, she knew the yo-yo tricks. When mom got wound up, she re-directed the situation. The dog leash hung by the front door for several "walk the doggies" every day. Mary Elizabeth made it possible for Mom to age in place. She became a calm presence, part of the daily fabric of my mother's life. They walked to the Y every morning, took water aerobics, and co-hosted the daily 5:00 p.m. dog parties. She made sure Mom was on the porch swing in the afternoon to greet the mailman and wave to the neighborhood children.

It was excruciating to say goodbye when my six-week visit ended. Mom's eyes still looked hollow, and they flooded with tears as we hugged. I felt numb. Three states and two time zones away, I struggled to find the emotional distance necessary to function without guilt. Would I ever see her again? With regular phone calls and copious cards we managed to stay in close touch, both of us hanging on.

Beloved Bundt Cake

Sarah Ohlin

"Milk shakes, fries, ramen noodles, ice cream, all the foods you would normally not eat for a healthy diet because they retain weight. These are the kinds of things you want to get her to eat. We're going to get her fattened up."

I had been furiously taking notes but at this I stopped and looked up. The hospital nutritionist had finished speaking in her high, happy voice. There was a huge smile on her face, as if we'd just discussed the menu for a birthday party instead of what foods would help my mother put on weight, because her Stage Four lung cancer was ravaging her body, and I was trying to keep her hydrated and fed.

In trying to keep up with the nutritionist's list, I'd missed the tone of her voice, but her last words, "Get her fattened up," shocked me out of my note-taking stupor. She sounded so happy, so airy, so positive that it made me feel sick to my stomach. Did she fail to see the gravity of situation? I was sure our goal was not to "get her fattened up," which sounded more like feeding a goose destined to be paté rather than a human. It was to get my mom some foods she could tolerate that might stay in her body instead of exploding out of her.

Quickly losing my calm to panic and anger, I wanted to shout, "Can you please stop calling my mother 'her'? She's sitting right here in the room with us, and you know her name is Mary!"

My sister, my mother, the nutritionist, a palliative care nurse, and I sat in an exam room at the shiny new cancer center, sleek and silvery on its exterior, with its mirrored windows. I looked around the oddly shaped room we occupied. My mom was expressionless and looked exhausted, the palliative care nurse wouldn't meet my eyes, and my sister reflected my own emotions; she was confused and scared. We both felt like we'd been hit by a Mack truck and didn't know if we'd survive the impact. We also didn't know that our mother would be dead two weeks later.

Just a few days earlier, the oncologist had given her six months to a year to live. Had we known death was so imminent, I might not have been so worried about what she was eating. In fact, had I known anything about the late stages of life, we wouldn't have been having this meeting. But I didn't know these things, so I was in pilot mode, flying a plane to an unknown destination, because that's what needed to be done; it was either stay aloft or crash. And at this point I still longed for my mother to be happy and healthy.

Why I was worried about *healthy* I don't know. I had seen the scans of her ravaged body, and the cancer was everywhere. Her colon was being eaten away by it; it was living in her bones, pressing painfully on her brain, and taking over her liver. My mother was about as far away from healthy as she could get, and there was clearly no way to bring her back. The only thing more stupid than worrying about keeping her healthy was thinking I could make her happy. But I was really scared. My fear was palpable, a living, physical pain in my chest, and feeding people was one powerful way I knew to bring comfort. I had learned this from a lifetime of my mom making delicious meals for everyone and from years of cooking with her. Cooking and enjoying food was an integral part of life for my family and me; it was virtually our second language. So I latched onto my need to feed my mother as a way of communicating with her and ignoring my fear.

Months before her diagnosis of lung cancer, I thought my mom was literally losing her mind. Alzheimer's and dementia began to enter my thoughts. But once I saw the CAT scans of her advanced cancer, her odd behavior, constantly upset stomach, and persistent cough all made sense. Then, during the weeks leading up to her death, Mom began to lose all interest in food. The months of watching her deterioration had been hard. But watching her lose interest in food and wine was a million times worse.

Two days after the meeting with the nutritionist, Mom shocked me by asking for cake. "I want chocolate cake. A real one," she said, "with real chocolate frosting."

Suddenly I had a mission. I researched highly rated bakeries in our area, not caring how expensive or how far away they were. I just wanted a cake that would be melt-in-your-mouth divine. I finally decided on a particular bakery and ordered a nine-inch, five-layer, classic chocolate cake. I couldn't wait for my mom to dig into it. This cake symbolized so much! She had specifically requested it after barely ingesting anything at all. I wanted her to love it, to ask for more, to put on weight, to flat out deny the cancer, to stay right where she was in my life for a very long time.

As it happens, my brother and I have birthdays a day apart, and for as long as I can remember we shared a birthday party. One year when we were kids, Mom made a chocolate chocolate chip bundt cake. It became our birthday tradition. Even when I went to college, Mom would make that cake and mail it to me.

This cake isn't fancy. It's doesn't represent a spectacular feat of baking requiring special flour or Swiss chocolate. But it is deliciously moistened with sour cream and oil in the batter, the chocolate isn't too sweet, and the nearly burnt edges against the rim of the pan add a touch of savory, smoky flavor. Topped with a light dusting of powdered sugar and cut into slices when the chocolate chips can still melt, it's a true treasure. I can taste that rich chocolate swimming on my tongue to this day.

My mother, an excellent cook, had other chocolate cake recipes, including Aunt Max's special one, but none was equal to her chocolate chocolate chip bundt cake. Over the years, other family members adopted the recipe, and we never tired of it. It was our go-to treat for all special occasions, symbolizing excellence in eating, family fun, and mutual comfort.

The minute I picked up the five-layer classic chocolate cake from the bakery and looked at its perfect, velvet brown elegance, I knew it was a mistake. It seemed preposterous. Suddenly I felt like the nutritionist with her saccharine voice in seeming denial of a serious situation. The cake, I thought, was a fraud, and so was I.

The few days between when Mom had requested the cake and the day I picked it up were drastic in terms of her diminished appetite. She tasted only a bite of the monstrous cake, I suspect simply to please me. Those of us present, I thought, would live with the lasting memory of her unhappily holding a plate full of over-the-top cake, while we raised forks full of this imposter and forced bits into our own mouths, along with the truth that she was dying. Eating fancy cake wasn't going to change a thing.

Until that moment, it had never occurred to me to bake our beloved chocolate chocolate chip bundt cake for my mother when she requested a cake. It was as if it never even existed. That it never occurred to me reveals how my brain was working or, more precisely, not working during those difficult days. *Don't think, don't feel, just do what needs to be done and what Mom's asking for.*

Don't think. Don't feel — two things I wish I had *known* to let go of. By attempting not to feel emotion I had excised parts of myself that probably should have been present at such an important and powerful time. Had I allowed myself to be emotional, perhaps the chocolate chocolate chip bundt cake, with all its love and warm memories, might have become one last special gift for my mom.

Or is it possible that our chocolate chocolate chip bundt cake might have been just as preposterous as the bakery cake four days before she died? Perhaps the real question is this: Had I fulfilled my role adequately in my mother's dying days? I suppose there will always be something I regret about those last few weeks, because in the end, no matter what I did or failed to do, whether denying my emotions or not baking the perfect chocolate cake, I simply couldn't save my mom.

Now, four years after her death, I can say that I'm glad our beloved bundt cake didn't appear during that dark struggle of Mom's last days. Instead, it can remain a part of the beloved, joyful, warm memories our extended family shares, grounded as always in tradition and connection and not a reminder of death knocking at our door.

Joyful Mystery

Patti See

My mom is in the hospital again for observation following a series of mini strokes. She did not want to go out like this: after she was diagnosed with Alzheimer's disease, she said she never wanted to burden her family or have a life in which she couldn't do what she liked.

I sit close to her bed and flip through TV channels. I settle on *Terminator 2*—not quite as dramatic on this tiny TV mounted in the far corner of the room. My mom hasn't been able to follow a storyline for about seven years now. Still, she understands the universal language of blowing stuff up. "Wow," she says periodically throughout Arnold Schwarzenegger's shootout sequences.

A cardiac technician wheels his portable echocardiogram into the room and asks if now is a good time. I mute the TV, and he attaches his round, sticky pads to my mom's chest, careful never to expose either breast. He talks to my mom about what he's doing. "She can't really communicate anymore," I tell him. Still, he says to her, "This echo will tell us if your heart is damaged."

She keeps her eyes on me and smiles. On the small monitor this grainy slug of my mother's heart looks like a gray hand flipping a middle finger with each quick beat. My eyes well as I watch in awe. How many of us have seen an ultrasound of our own unborn babies, but few have an opportunity to view a parent's beating heart. "Everything looks just fine," the technician says. I cry some more. She could linger like this for many years. Alzheimer's teaches us there are possibilities worse than death.

My mom can no longer walk independently, and we know that eventually she will lose the ability to smile, to swallow, to speak. This prompted me to record my parents' voices starting a few years ago. I hold my MP-3 player in my hand, and its small size means my recordings are more like a casual visit than an awkward interview. Though I have prepared questions to ask my dad ("What were your jobs on the farm as a kid?" or "What surprised you about the way your life turned out?"), mostly my recordings are daily adventures of an octogenarian couple and their adult daughter. On one I'm mixing cookies, narrating as I stir, while my mom has a conversation with the button on her sweater and my dad reads the grocery store flyer aloud to us. On another my mom sings along with a Christmas album. She doesn't know her own name, but she can sing "Adeste Fidelis" entirely in Latin. Today in the hospital I contemplate that I may never hear my mother speak a coherent sentence again.

After the technician wheels away his equipment, the breakfast tray arrives, and I coax my mom into eating a few bites of waffle. I narrate just as I do with her at home: "Look, syrup in a little square container. You like syrup."

She doesn't know what to do with the straw in her mouth, and she has trouble swallowing. Finally I give up feeding her and flip through channels.

I stop when I get to nuns. My mom perks up as soon as she sees them. We join the Rosary in progress, in the midst of the Joyful Mystery. The nuns are in full regalia, and for a moment I can't think of what their outfits are called. I might have twelve years of Catholic school behind me, but today I'm functioning on too little sleep. My mind is murky.

Mom hasn't spoken much beyond "wow" in almost 24 hours. Now she says the prayers with these church channel nuns, as real to her as if they were in the same room with us. She says the

Apostles' Creed, Our Father, Hail Mary, the Glory Be. She knows every word.

My mom fingers the edge of her blankets, I suspect looking for her rosary beads. All of her life she prayed the Rosary in bed, in her living room rocker, at the kitchen table. She believed that on every road trip, praying the Rosary kept our car from a head-on collision or that every pregnancy — her own eight and her children's sixteen — produced a healthy child because of her daily devotions. "I never lost a one," she often said to me. She put her entire life in the hands of God, and she found comfort in the power of her Rosary.

Now, the more prayers she says, the louder her voice becomes. I hold her hand. So much amazes me: her strong heart, her stronger faith, these lessons she still continues to teach me. "Habit," I say out loud to my mother. "Look, they're in their full habits."

One Saturday, months before Mom's mini-strokes brought her to the hospital, I'm recording our conversation while her Big Band album plays in the background. She breaks into song … 'It's been a wrong, wrong time.' I say, "I think it's 'long, long time.'" We have listened to this album every Saturday for almost three years now. Our pattern is that I give her a bath after breakfast, and we listen to music in the living room until naptime. She belts out, "Lick me once, and lick me twice, and lick me once again."

I burst into laughter. "It's 'kiss,' you goof." I laugh some more. "Kitty Kallen couldn't sing 'lick me' on the radio in 1945."

"They can get licks in there too" she argues. "Some of the kids do that." She keeps singing, "Kiss me once, and kiss me twice, then kiss me once again. It's been a long, long time."

"I bet you were quite the kisser," I say.

"Uh-uh. I love it."

I laugh until I cry. A daughter's joy. A mother's mystery.

For awhile, I believe that the last time I'll ever hear my mom speak a full sentence was when she prayed with nuns on TV. Besides making a pretty good story, it truly comforts me. When she gets out of the hospital, I decide to cancel my spring break trip to New Orleans, which is set for a few days later. My trip insurance requires me to contact her doctor about signing paperwork to confirm that yes indeed my mom did suffer a series of transient ischemic attacks (TIA) or mini strokes. My call to her doctor leads to a "prescription" for hospice for Mom. "It's time," his kind nurse says to me on the phone.

My dad thinks hospice care is just for "people who are dying." I say gently, "Mom's doctor must think she qualifies. Hospice is for people who have less than six months to live."

Her diagnosis eight years ago gave us ellipses: Mom will die from Alzheimer's…

Hospice offers us a period: Mom will die from Alzheimer's.

This could be over within six months, a strange comfort.

A week later, on Easter Sunday—which happens to be a day after my mom's 81st birthday—my sister and I plan to give Mom a bath while my dad is at church. We walk her to the bathroom to get her cleaned up after breakfast. "You okay, Mama?" I ask.

She shakes her head. I swear she says, "I don't know who I am."

"Did you hear that?" I ask Ger.

"She never said anything like that before," Ger says.

We get her full diaper off and plant her on the toilet topper, impossible without dirtying both of her legs. Like changing your baby's diaper, the only ones that faze you after awhile are the especially "heavy" ones. This one qualifies. Once she's on the toilet topper, her whole body goes limp, her tongue comes out, and her eyes roll. We recognize that she is having another TIA. When she was in the hospital, her doctor said that eventually these smaller strokes might lead to a big one, from which she will never recover. Blood flow to her brain will simply stop. Both of us have to balance Mom, or she'd slide off the toilet. We've got to clean her up before we can do anything. Ger wipes Mom's butt and legs and hums "Here Comes Peter Cotton Tail." She wipes and hums, hums and wipes. She goes through baby wipe after baby wipe, a little like trying to clean up an oil spill with a hankie. At some point I slip out of my Easter dress and rummage through my mom's closet for a T-shirt to go over my leggings and tank top.

Mom's eyes are still closed. She inhales two big breaths and then—nothing. We steady her on the toilet. "I think she's dying," I say. We hear a kerplunk. Perhaps it's her body flushing before she dies. All I can think is, "Well, here we go."

I look at my watch. 11:15. We have at least 45 minutes to decide what to do before my dad gets home from church. Should we call an ambulance or let her go? I call my brother, Joe, a firefighter and EMT. He picks up his cell phone on the second ring. He's at the fire station. He says that if Mom is having another TIA, it will pass. If it's the big one, just let her be. "But what should we *do*?" I say. He tells us to lay her on the floor. When I get off the phone, Ger says, "Isn't he coming?" We're both a little desperate. I can't imagine being here without her. I say, "Only if we call the ambulance. He can't leave work unless he's responding to a call."

We get Mom mostly cleaned up and slide her onto the bathroom floor on a large bath towel. Somehow we get another diaper on her and a pair of sweat pants. She's still wearing her pink flannel pajama top. We roll up a towel and put it beneath her head for a pillow. We wait. She's breathing softly, and her eyes are closed. Ger and I stand in the hallway next to the open bathroom door and talk about people we know who died on the pot. Definitely not the way we want to go, we both agree. We tell each other—if we get Alzheimer's—how each of us will off herself so her family doesn't have to deal with this. One opts for pills, another for drowning. I tell my sister something I haven't said to any family member: If Mom were a dog, we would have taken her to the vet for a much more humane ending than this. I paraphrase a poem I read recently: "Sometimes death is not as terrible as denying it."

It occurs to me that perhaps Mom can still hear us. I wouldn't put it past her, coming back from the dead because she was pissed at what we were saying. I put my Easter dress back on and find my camera in the pocket. We move to the living room and leave her on the bathroom floor with the door wide open so we can hear her. Ger's husband shows up to help us move Mom, but we decide to leave her on the floor till the rest of the family arrives. I tell Tim, "Ger was so calm. She just kept humming 'Here Comes Peter Cotton Tail' through it all."

"I did not," she says.

"Yes. You did. You hummed as you cleaned up Mom. I thought you were doing it to keep us both calm." She giggles a little bit.

I say to Tim, "I leave the room to strip out of my nice dress so I don't get poop on it, and I come back and Ger is still humming." I sing in a falsetto voice, "Here comes Peter Cotton Tail, hoppin' down the bunny trail. Hippity hoppity Easter's on its way."

She and I laugh hysterically. It never occurred to me hers was a nervous hum, an Easter- and stroke- and shit-induced tick. We can barely catch our breath.

Around 12:15 my dad and the rest of the family come home from church. We give them the short version of what transpired, minus Peter Cotton Tail. My dad says, "So do you think she can take Communion?" Each Sunday he brings a blessed host home for Mom and coaxes her into swallowing it. "I don't think just yet," I say. I know how important this is to him, especially on Easter. My mom believed wholeheartedly in the Resurrection, our foundation of faith as Catholics.

My brother picks Mom up from the bathroom floor and puts her in her wheelchair. Ger and I put a clean sweatshirt on her. She seems more alert than she was right after her TIA, but she still can't do anything but stare into space.

Here's what I love about my family: Perhaps only one of them would say, "Yeah, Ma just had a stroke, but we've got this birthday cake for her already made so let's prop her up at the table for awhile." We light the candles on her cake, and we all sing Happy Birthday to her and take pictures. Then we lay her down for a nap, and she sleeps the rest of the day.

Hours later—after Easter dinner and birthday cake and family small talk and washing many dishes—I say quietly to Ger, "I still feel like I could throw up."

"Oh," she says, "just put lotion on your hands, and the smell will go away."

"Not the poop," I say, "everything."

I go home and burn winter debris in my yard. Twigs and leaves and last year's stalks dried into the ground, anything I can find. A fire is cleansing, therapeutic.

That night I turn on my computer to upload the day's photographs from my camera. While I'm waiting, I open an email from Ger: "Guess what I just found on my jeans? Poop. I bet it was there all day. Don't laugh or I'll sing 'Here Comes Peter Cotton Tail' again." I laugh and laugh. Then my photos appear on the screen. I have no memory of taking my mom's picture when she was lying on the bathroom floor, but obviously I must have thought it was a good idea.

When I see her, I am reminded of the photos my parents had in their attic: dead relatives laid out in their caskets at their wakes. When I was a kid, I remember my mom telling me that back then—in the 1930's and 40's—there were so few family members with access to a camera that they wanted to capture a loved one in their casket to have it as a keepsake. I didn't know the word "macabre" as a kid, but I knew the feeling I got when I looked at those photos, the same feeling I have now when I see my mom laid out, towel headrest, pajama-top sloppily tucked into her brown sweat pants, her eyes slits, her hands folded in what I can only describe as *in prayer*.

Mothering My Mother

Weam Namou

It's 2:04 am, and, once again, I am up in the middle of the night, listening to my eighty-two year-old mother's loud gurgling sound, which sounds like a death rattle, from the adjacent room. Tears run down my face as I wonder, will today be her last day on earth? I get a few hours of sleep before it's time to wake up and get my children ready for school.

My son, a kindergartner, cries, "I don't want to go to school! It's boring!"

My daughter, a third grader, wants to wear a fancy dress with ruffles. I explain that this dress is not appropriate for school. She throws a tantrum, my son continues with his "School is boring!" mantra and then my husband appears.

"I'm going to be late for work," he says. "If they're not ready in five minutes, I'm leaving without them, and you'll have to drop them off at school."

I toss out all my niceties and start hollering demands until the kids are dressed, lunches are packed, and everyone is out of the house. Once I close the door, I inhale the silence as though it's oxygen I have not had for days. I make myself a cup of coffee and sit at my computer to write. I'm a writer, and that's one of the reasons my mother is living with me. Aside from needing someone to take care of her, she needs the type of supervision that fits the lifestyle of a writer with children who loves to stay home.

Within less than a year, my mother had fallen twice, had surgery, become a disabled dementia patient, and had to be admitted to a short-term rehab center/nursing home. There, she lost her spirit. She became unrecognizable to us, and we became unrecognizable to her. When her release date approached, the only one of her ten children who offered to take her in already had a handicapped husband to care for at home. The last time she tried to take my mother in, the situation was unbearably chaotic and unsafe for my sister and for my mother.

The idea that my mother would remain in a nursing home, the last place she ever thought she'd be, distressed our family. We were all born in Baghdad, Iraq, as Chaldeans (Christian Iraqis). Chaldeans trace their ancestors to Prophet Abraham, as he was born in Ur, land of the Chaldees. Our tribal upbringing is thousands of years old, and to break it now, by forcing my mother into a western system, meant a great dishonor for her and us. It was as if we were signing her death warrant.

My mother got married at age twelve and had twelve children, two of whom died young. She has more than thirty grandchildren and almost a dozen great-grandchildren. She does not know how to read or write, she does not speak English, and she has never worked outside of her home. The only thing she knows is home.

"What are we going to do about Mom?" we asked each other, feeling guilt and confusion. No one had an answer.

At night, I could not sleep. My conscience gnawed at me. I thought of taking her in, but I had waited all these years for my children to start school full-time, so I could focus on my writing, and now that the time had come, the idea of being a caregiver frightened me. My siblings offered to help whoever took her in, but the way I saw it, that was part of the problem. Helping mom meant no privacy for me. My house would turn into a coffee shop.

I prayed about the matter and went to church. One Sunday, the pastor's sermon was about acting in a loving way now, not waiting until it's too late. It felt as though his words were directed at me. I closed my eyes and thought about our family story and the legacy I wanted to leave behind. I walked out of church that day with tears in my eyes and a sense of assurance from a higher power that I would receive sufficient help. The journey was in place.

* * * * *

The phone rings. It's Doctor Bakker, the tall and skinny podiatrist with white hair who reminds me of a mad scientist. He has been working on my mother's left foot, because it has a bedsore that was healing from her last hospital stay. "How's your mother doing?" he asks.

"She was in the emergency room a few days ago."

"She was?"

"The visiting doctor thought she had pneumonia, so she sent her to the ER. The ambulance picked her up and, later that same day, the ER doctor released her. He said all the tests came back negative."

"Hmmm, that's peculiar."

Initially, I was happy to hear that, but now I'm worried again. "Her rattling hasn't gone away, and she's behaving strangely. Yesterday she did not want to lie down and asked me to take her outside. Usually she's tired and prefers staying inside." I had read that people, when they near death, have a sudden burst of energy.

"Do you think I can see her in about half an hour?" he asks.

"Yes. She's still sleeping, but it's noon, so I should get her up."

She's so weak today that I'm not sure if I'll be able to get her safely into the wheelchair. Normally she helps a little. That part goes well, and, after her toiletry, I bring her to the kitchen table and place the usual breakfast in front of her, sliced Spanish cheese and tomatoes, pita bread, and a cup of tea and milk. I clear some dirty dishes, pick up Lego pieces and school papers from the floor, and make myself another cup of coffee. When I glance in her direction, I notice she cannot lift the Spanish cheese slice to her mouth. It's hanging by her fingers in midair. Her expressionless face and droopy mouth worry me.

"Mom, what's wrong?" I ask.

"I'm tired," she says, her voice exhausted.

I remove the breakfast for fear she will choke on it. By the time I'm done, she's fast asleep. There's a knock on the door, and I open it quickly, knowing it is Doctor Bakker.

I welcome him inside and prepare the items that he normally needs, like disposable bed pads to place under her foot and a Styrofoam cup with half an inch of water in it. As he digs out the dead skin with his scalpel, my mother continues to sleep. Dr. Bakker says, "She must be really tired from the last two days' excitement."

An hour passes, and she's still asleep. After he leaves, I try to wake her up but to no avail. She does not respond. In times like this, I wonder, is this her time to go? Should I honor that this is the case or try to revive her? Since she moved into my home, she has, on several occasions, told me that she wanted to die. Twice or three times, she called me to sit in front of her because, she said, "I'm going to die."

I obliged, sat in front of her, and cried my eyes out for hours as I awaited her death. Yet she remained alive for days, weeks, and months. Evidently there was a miscommunication between her and the spirit world, a realm she visits often. I know this, because, every now and then, when she opens her eyes from a long, deep sleep, I see tears. I ask her whom has she seen in her dream, and she says sadly, but with exquisite memory, "Your father and my tribe."

I ask if she would like to leave this earth and go to the other world. She says, "Yes, why not? Whatever God prefers."

I move her to her bed and pick up the kids at school. When they enter the house and don't see her lying on the couch, where she normally is, they ask, "Where's Nana?"

"She's tired," I say. "She's in her bed."

I check on my mother, and she looks comatose. I don't know what to do, whether or not to call the family. A knock on the door startles me.

"Who is it?" I ask.

"It's Stella."

Relieved to hear the nurse's voice, I quickly open the door. "It's so good to see you!"

"I know I didn't call," she says. "I was in the area, and I knew you get home at this time after you pick up the kids from school. So I thought I'd check on your mom, since she just got out of the hospital. How is she doing?"

"Not too good."

"What's wrong?"

I lead her to the bedroom, and she takes my mother's vitals and looks into her eyes. Stella is a Native American with long hair, long nails, and a long nursing career. She cared for her mother for thirty years. She says, reluctantly, "It doesn't look too good. It's a matter of a few days, maybe less…"

I break down crying, and my daughter appears and hugs me. What's wrong, mommy?" she asks.

"Nana might not stay with us for long."

"No, mom! No! I want her to stay!"

She bursts into tears, deeper than I expect from her.

"Don't be sad," I say to her. "That's what Nanna wants. She wants to go and be in peace with God and to see my Babba, her husband, and the rest of her family."

"Don't you have a sister there too?" she asks.

I pause, and then I remember my deceased sister. "Yes, I do. They've all been waiting for her a long time, and now it's their turn to spend time with her."

My daughter cries even harder. I hug and kiss her.

"We're lucky we had this time with her," I say. "She gave me many gifts, and living with us was one of her biggest gifts."

The nurse says I'd better tell the family, so we can decide whether to take her to the hospital or leave her at home. When Stella leaves, I call my sisters. They come one by one, sad and distraught. One breaks into loud crying. I ask her please to stop. "You're scaring mom!" I say.

45

My brothers then start arriving, followed by my nieces and nephews. One niece and nephew encourage us to take my mother to the hospital. I explain that she was just there, and they found nothing wrong with her. I'm afraid she will die there. We argue about whether the wisest choice is to handle this medically or to allow nature to take its course. In the end, I call her visiting doctor to relay the situation. "I can't believe the ER sent her back without giving her anything," she says. "I'm going to prescribe an antibiotic. Give her two today and then one every day until it's done."

She calls in the prescription, and I make it to the pharmacy minutes before they close. I give my mother the medicine, everyone goes home, and I call a friend in another state who volunteers for hospice. I want to learn more about this service, in case we need it.

The next day is hectic again. Family arrives early in the morning, and I have to interview someone for my book in the afternoon. I escape the house at the appointed interview time, unable to handle my mother lying in her death bed and the number of people coming and going in my home.

When I return, I find everyone laughing and joking. "She's doing real good!" my sister says. "She ate biscuits and drank milk. I fed her the soup I brought. She's looking at us, smiling, and she even said a few words!"

I almost pass out with relief and anxiety. Over the course of two years, my mother has had a number of near-death experiences which completely drained me. I think I cannot handle another episode, and I wonder how many more are to come.

The nurse visits the next day. When I tell her what happened, she observes my mother with a smile. "The other day when I left your house and went home, I told my husband that that poor woman would last only a few hours and that her family might not make it in time to see her. All her vitals indicated that. For her to turn around within a matter of days is nothing short of a miracle. I've been a nurse for more than forty years, and I've never seen someone rally like that. I don't think the antibiotic did that. Something else made it happen."

She's right, I think. Having her children around her, praying for her and asking her to stay, maybe my mother did not want to go after all.

That weekend forces me to make changes. I decide that no matter what happens, I will not think about my mother's death or allow myself to be fazed by her condition. I also decide to take better care of myself. I begin to take long walks, do yoga more regularly, and ask for help without fear of inconveniencing anyone. I set boundaries. I tell my siblings that having too many visitors strains me and that if they wish to visit our mother they have to find alternative ways, perhaps taking her to their home for a few hours, even if transportation is difficult.

"God bless you and your children!" my mother says in her quivering voice whenever I put her to bed at night. I smile at her. In our culture, we believe taking care of a parent is an honor and a blessing. I know that, despite the challenges, my mother's presence deeply enriches our lives.

Lessons from My Mother: Communicating with Someone You Love Who Has Alzheimer's Disease

Helen Dening

Fear, uncertainty, and pain are words often associated with Alzheimer's Disease, the sixth leading cause of death in the US, affecting more than five million people and their families. It cannot be cured or prevented. It's a terrible, mind-destroying disease.

My mother, once a remarkable, determined woman, has Alzheimer's. She and my father had six children and owned a sizeable poultry farm. Now, my mother's competence and passion for life have disappeared. So have her abilities to walk and speak coherently. As her mind continues to be snatched away, I search for ways to slow the process—and for ways to calm her fears and anxieties (and mine).

I look for ways to communicate with words and actions that are loving and respectful. My attempts remind me of communicating with young children. Both my mother and young children are trying to make sense of their world. Both are experiencing "newness." Both need repetition in order to build memory. Strategies I have learned while working more than twenty years with young children are now valuable in assisting my mother. If your loved one has early stages of Alzheimer's, perhaps these tips will be useful.

1. Show, Don't Tell

It is difficult to expect someone to perform a task when the person no longer knows what the task is, no longer remembers the steps necessary for completing the task, or when the words you're speaking seem foreign. This leads to frustration and anxiety. Show your loved one how to perform a task by completing it together. Life-care skills such as dressing, combing hair, setting the table, or sweeping may need to be modeled and/or assisted. You may have to repeat the process each time as if it's the first time. There may be no memory of the activity or how to carry it out.

2. Modify and Simplify Favorite Activities

Favorite activities may become confusing and difficult. Card games, even children's card games, may no longer be options. Laminate old photographs, postcards, or magazine pictures. These may become favorites, with your loved one spending long amounts of time "studying" them. The person or places in the photo may be unknown. Studying the photos helps reclaim memories. And old postcard of a mountain scene may trigger memories of vacations in the mountains.

3. Following Directions

Alzheimer victims lose their ability to follow a series of directions. Give one direction, and wait for it to be completed before giving another direction. Keep the direction simple and the details broken down into manageable steps. I used to ask simple questions requiring a choice: "Do you want to take your coat off? What would you like to eat?" only to discover that I was adding to the stress. Now there are fewer questions and more directing. "Let's take your coat off. Here's a hanger to put your coat on."

4. Listen with Patience

My mother's thoughts, once expressed in complete sentences, have become jumbled words and phrases. Now, careful listening is required to interpret the meaning behind the single word, gestures, or utterances. As the ability to verbally communicate decreases, your need to express love, patience, and understanding increases.

5. Look for Nonverbal Cues

Nonverbal cues are important when verbally expressed feelings, needs, or desires are difficult or impossible to understand. Sometimes your body language speaks volumes when there are no words. I have found that agitation, fears, and tears can be calmed by holding a hand or giving a hug. A hug speaks louder than words. Redirecting my mother's focus and compassionately reassuring her that she is safe and loved helps alleviates those difficult moments.

* * * * *

I would love for things to be as they once were. I want to bake apple pies with my mother, sit with her in her garden, laugh over family stories, and have our special "Girls' day out." All this is gone. My mother still enjoys our outings, but they require creative planning, because surrounding noises and distractions increase her confusion and fears.

Alzheimer's disease destroys more than the victim. It spreads into families and communities, often leaving a trail of hopelessness and helplessness. I continually seek options for communicating with my mother. As the disease claims more of her, my means and strategies for communicating with her will change. For now, these strategies help make the moments with my mother more loving, meaning, and understandable.

New Horizons

Deborah Marshall

Reception smiles, nods.
The long hallway swallows me.
Her head pops out, bobs.

Each door boasts loudly:
retired police shield, wreath,
dream-catcher, a flag.

Her door sports nothing.
She retreats from her threshold.
"Finally, you're here."

Housekeeping's been in.
The smell of cleansers loiters.
The toilet sparkles.

"The only good thing
about this place is leaving."
Her earrings don't match.

We walk to my car.
"So good to escape this jail.
Cripples and crazies."

The playlist begins:
"I only moved here for you.
No one says hello.

"There's nothing to do.
Activities are a joke.
I have ten doctors.

"The social worker
is easy to talk to, but
what's she gonna do?

"I never want those
fat lazy aides helping me.
I'm not a racist.

"That maid never dusts.
Meals really have gone downhill.
Desserts were good once.

"I've had a wonderful life.
Blind, deaf and crippled.
I should get a cat.

"That podiatrist!
What a racket he has here.
Ten minute sessions.

"What if I can't put
the new hearing aids in?
More money wasted.

"Every night I pray that
God takes me in my sleep
before I go blind.

"I'll be eighty-nine.
Good your father never knew
you put me in here."

Handicapped parking
is a perk. Once in Target
I struggle to trail her

and her cart crashing,
Mr. Magoo on a spree:
Cortizone ointment,

Kleenex and cream cheese.
She hands the clerk one dollar
instead of a twenty.

The playlist repeats:
"I have nothing to live for.
Screw the golden years.

"Why do people think
it's good to live a long time?
All your friends die.

"I'm still mad at you.
I could drive during the day.
I wouldn't at night.

"I'm so depressed.
Those anti-anxiety meds
are not working.

"I heard on TV
what's most aging is gray hair,
then weight, then a cane.

"You're awfully quiet.
Why shouldn't I get a cat,
an old indoor cat?

"When will you be back?
Don't forget my dirty clothes.
There's a lot this week.

"I'm on fourteen meds.
Have you heard from your brother?
Call me this weekend.

"I pray your children
never put you in a place
like this. You don't know."

The Weekly Round

Deborah Marshall

"Stop yelling at me."
I implore the insertion
of new hearing aids.

Weekly rituals:
Identify found objects.
Pluck her stray whiskers.

Check the thermostat.
Sort, read her mail. Take all bills.
Reset remotes, clocks.

Although the house van
drives residents for shopping
(to Walmart one week;

next week to Kappy's,
TJX, Sudbury Farms)
weekly, I indulge

her addiction. Trips
to Kohl's, the Christmas Tree Shop
or Market Basket.

We triangulate
among doctors, pharmacists
and more therapists.

Weekly, I bleach, wash,
and fold soiled underwear.
Stains fade, but remain.

I return clean clothes.
What plenary indulgence
may I hope for?

"I know why you are
depressed. You're guilty you
put me in this place."

Been Writing?

Deborah Marshall

She had meant poems.
I softly uttered, "A bit."
Not one poem all year.

But I had written:
monthly emails alerting
of my dad's decline;

For the Boston Globe
obituary factoids
priced by the word;

A quick toast for Pa
casket-side during the wake
with shots of whisky;

His church eulogy
with a five minute limit,
the monsignor's rule;

Many thank you notes
on behalf of my mother
who's legally blind;

Notifications
to Social Security,
his pension, cable,

phone, bank, credit cards,
attorney, the registry,
and insurances.

I write my dad's name
in the sand at low tide.
Mostly, I write checks.

Lines

Rosa Smith

We see lines
spun strong by flax and grit
embedded on an ancient forehead
like a firing squad lining up to pierce our hearts
one day.

Lines can be soft
like sugar syrup in the thread stage.
Some of us can hanker for a line of cocaine
others a line of credit.
We line up for the bus home at the end of a long day
and we die in the line of duty.
We cheer when our team gets a single on a line drive
and if we are actors we memorize our lines.

We can even imagine toeing the line
in the British Royal Navy,
building the Maginot Line
between France and Germany
or discussing psychology with Jung and Freud,
but our brains turn to ashes and dust
when we try to remember
the timeline
of our mother's decline.

PART TWO

The Men in our Lives

Being my Dad's Many-Daughters

Ellen Meeropol

Over a decade ago, I moved my elderly parents to an independent living apartment fifteen minutes from my Massachusetts home. The move, a response to my mother's diagnosis of Alzheimer's disease, came as I was transitioning from a career as a nurse practitioner to working full time as a novelist. I was about to take early retirement from the hospital where I had worked for 24 years and was finishing a graduate program in fiction writing. I stood on the brink of a new literary life, and the timing of my parents' move seemed perfect. I would have a more flexible schedule to help them settle into their new lives. I could happily be their writer-daughter.

Within four years of their move, I sold my first novel, and my mother died. My father, blind from a progressive, genetic retinal disease, had never learned to use Braille or a white cane; Mom had been his eyes for more than 60 years. He wanted to stay in their apartment, so he learned to use a white cane. I did his laundry and grocery shopping, but otherwise he was self-reliant – making his own breakfast and lunch, walking to the dining room for dinner. He wasn't very good with the cane, but his neighbors learned to get out of his way. He used the treadmill in the exercise room daily and listened to Talking Books for entertainment and keeping up with the world. For a blind man in his 90's, he was healthy and independent.

With the flexibility of my writing schedule, I was able to visit him frequently. My medical background helped him negotiate the health care system and get what he needed. Over the next seven years, Dad and I became closer. He embraced my new career. When my first novel was published, I recorded it and had it converted to a digital Talking Book for Dad to read, even though he prefers science fiction. I was able to fill the roles of writer-daughter and nurse-daughter with some modicum of grace. Dad and I got along well, but we rarely discussed the issue that divided us more than any other: political activism.

My parents were liberals. Like many of my generation, I felt that their liberal analysis and actions didn't go far enough to address racial, economic and gender injustice. My political activism – in civil rights, the women's movement, and against the Vietnam War – made my parents very nervous. These differences came to a head one May evening in 1970, after a big anti-war protest in Washington. My husband and our friends were in sleeping bags in the basement of my parents' house. I sat in the living room with my father, explaining that the demonstration had been much more confrontational than previous ones. It was the first time I heard the term "trashing" to describe politically motivated destruction of property. I was excited about the energy of the angry demonstrators and frightened about the tactical escalation. My dad didn't say much.

"If I acted on my strong political beliefs, and did something illegal at one of these demonstrations," I asked him, "and I had to go underground, would you hide me?"

He hesitated before answering. "No."

I didn't know how to respond. Did he just want me to think seriously about actions and consequences? If I came to him in trouble and asked him to put aside his own political beliefs and help me, did he really mean that he would turn me in?

Maybe he did mean it. In the tumultuous years of the late 1960s and early 1970s, my father and I agreed about little politically. Because his blindness had made him unable to continue his work as a lab chemist, he was transferred into administration positions in the federal agency where he worked. He was smart and talented and was soon the chief of a division dealing with setting standards for police equipment. He didn't tell me about that promotion for several years after it happened; he knew my low opinion of cops.

Over the decades, my father's opinions about the world have shifted substantially to the left. By the time he moved to Massachusetts, we agreed much more than we did in 1970. But although we frequently discussed politics and the abysmal state of the world, we never explicitly returned to that May 1970 conversation. I have wondered about that exchange many times. It is no doubt a contributing thread to my ongoing fascination with the rich ground of political activism and family loyalties and to the fabric of the stories and novels I write.

Eighteen months ago, my father's usually robust physical health started to deteriorate. A spontaneous fracture produced chronic pain, which led to inactivity (no more walking to the dining hall with his white cane; no more treadmill) and then to a blood clot in his leg. We all know the story, how medical issues can escalate and cascade. "O.D.T.A.A.," my dad calls it. One Damn Thing After Another. Complicated by Dad's blindness and hearing loss, his sense of isolation and his frustration were significant. Dealing with his health problems was also overwhelming to me, as I tried to sandwich readings and book promotion events for my second novel in among multiple doctors' appointments and Dad's increased needs for my presence. As my father's carefully constructed independence was challenged, so was the delicate balance of our relationship.

Then things got worse. At age 98, my father spent July, August and September shuttling back and forth – by ambulance – among the medical center emergency room and various surgical procedures and a rehab nursing facility. His medical problems became even more tangled and complicated, requiring consultations with multiple physicians. Each specialist had a wildly different set of recommendations, and only one had the patience to speak slowly and loudly to a blind and mostly deaf man. I spent almost every day with my father as translator, nurse, and protector.

The medical decisions required were complex and difficult, making my daughter roles feel at war with each other. Nurse-daughter wanted to keep dad healthy and secure. I looked at his various impairments and couldn't imagine him safely returning to his apartment to live alone. Activist-daughter wanted to take on the medical establishment for treating him with so little respect, stripping him of his dignity.

Writer-daughter turned to a book, Atul Gawande's *Being Mortal: Medicine and What Matters in the End.* Reading this book, as my daughter-selves battled internally about how best to help my father, affected me profoundly. Gawande's emphasis on listening to what the ill person wants, to what is critically important to each individual, is something I already knew as a person and a nurse, but I needed this author's eloquent prose to break through my bossy-daughter self and listen to my dad.

My father moved back to his apartment and returned to living independently. His complicated medical status required more help from the Independent Living staff than previously and more of me. Professionally, I knew those caretaking tasks well, both the hands-on and the advocate parts. This new relationship led to greater father-daughter intimacy, but it also generated some conflict.

At 98, my father is still mentally sharp. He wants to be fully in charge of his health care decisions. I have to frequently tell nurse-daughter to back off and admonish activist-daughter to respect Dad's decisions. Of course, writer-daughter is always in the background, making notes.

I'm left with the just-daughter role, not an easy one for me. It requires taking a back seat to my dad's wishes, even when I think he's wrong. I don't fill this role gracefully.

Not long ago, I was having lunch with my father at his kitchen table in his apartment. Our conversation bounced back and forth between discussing the latest outrageous cop murder of a black teenager and arguing about how much time Dad should spend elevating his swollen legs. It struck me that perhaps he and I have been obliquely continuing that long-ago conversation, about supporting those we love in their choices even when those choices make us uncomfortable. In that often-indirect mode of family communication, Dad asking me to help him return to his home, in spite of my misgivings about that choice, echoed my long-ago request to him.

The realization made me feel better about my father's situation; it is precarious, and it has risks, but the risks are *his*. But the thing is, I still don't know whether or not my dad would turn me in.

An Answer and a Lesson

McClaren Malcolm

It began innocently. Dad had been slowing down, and he hadn't had a physical examination in some time. Mother scheduled a doctor's appointment for a routine exam, and I went along for moral support. The nurse asked Dad to sit on the examining table. When he had difficulty understanding her directions, she helped him up. "You're doing fine, Mr. Peterson."

He looked at her for a moment and then smiled. Engaging his droll wit, he said, "If I'm doing so fine, what am I doing here?"

A few days later, the doctor called with the CAT scan report. "Mr. Peterson has half the brain mass of a normal male his age. My diagnosis is senile dementia, suspected Alzheimer's."

If he said more than that, I didn't hear, because somewhere a steel door slammed. I swallowed hard. I knew little about Alzheimer's; I did know there was no cure. I heard myself asking, "How much time does he have?"

"We don't know, but you might find a care home for him soon."

Our family had had its crises: my divorce, Dad's bungled eye surgery. And yet we were strong survivors. We could get from dark to light; but this! There would be no cheerful greeting cards for him saying, "Hope you get well soon."

This was not what I wanted for him. He should read his paper in the morning, discuss politics with me in the afternoon, fly kites with his grandchildren on weekends, waltz with my mother on anniversaries. Then some night in the far future, when he was ready, he could go to his reward for a life well-lived. Instead he was sliding down a sink hole, soon unreachable, leaving Mother and me behind. No longer would we be the three bears. I felt the knife-edge of pain and worse---no hope.

Shortly after that phone call, we moved Dad to a care home. When he had good days, it was hard to believe his diagnosis. It made it harder to hear his question, "When can I come home?" Then I saw the bad days.

Let me take you back. As I enter his room, I wonder, who is he now? Dementia lurks in the back of his brain; it clouds his memory, short-circuits relationships, distorts his vision. He looks in the mirror and sees someone else, an older man, the man-in-the-wall. He talks to the man-in-the-wall. The man-in-the-wall lip-syncs what he says, but Dad doesn't notice.

Who is he now when he reaches out to me? He looks up from his wheel chair, his face open, loving, even joyful. Dad wants to hear how I am, what I'm doing. He talks to me about Louie. What do I know about Louie? I tell him what he told me years ago when I found his brother's picture in a photo album. "Louie looks like your brother Ed, Dad. He wanted to be a lawyer, and he was only sixteen when he collapsed and died from a stroke at his school desk."

"Oh," he says. "He went so quick. I don't remember him."

"You were only six."

"Don't you remember him?" he asks.

"I'm not your sister; I'm your daughter."

He looks puzzled. "I don't know about that," he says.

Pain dots my eyes as I hold back tears. My heart knots into a charley horse.

"I'm your daughter." My words sound thick and lumpy. His blank eyes look away. "Would you like some ice water, Dad?" I emphasize his relational name, "Dad."

"That would be nice." He settles into his chair with arms resting on his bubble tummy, fingers interlaced.

I rush out of his room and down the hall, releasing my tears. My tears belong here with the vegetable people, drooping in their wheelchairs scattered along the tunnel hall.

In a flood of feelings, I ask myself, why should a good man suffer indignities of pokes, prods, soiled diapers, public nudity? And how can I help when I recoil from touching his thorny hands and feet, or breathing the same heavy air he exhales, smelling the odious smells of Alzheimer's seeping from him, the smells that no bathing can remove?

I raise a prayer. "What must happen before he can die? What must I learn before he can go? What is the answer? Tell me, so I can do it and release him from his fatherly duties"---as though it were something so simple that I could control.

However simplistic, on the day I asked those questions, I took responsibility for his release, because I didn't know what else to do. If I was to have some role in his passing, I wanted to make sure I wasn't holding him up. If I had a lesson to learn, I wanted to get on with it. In the meantime, I could make a bad situation better, give my dad comfort in spite of my discomfort with his dying body. Gradually, quiet settled my inner spaces; a sad acceptance of my human limitations sifted in and gave me the strength to care for him.

Surely the nursing home must have a care plan in place for Dad. The home was high on the doctor's recommended list, so my expectations were high, too. Where to begin? The nurse sitting at her station looked starched and competent. No help was needed from me. Self-talk clicked in to bolster my resolve: Wasn't I right to oversee Dad's care, to be an advocate for him? Weren't his health and comfort the primary concerns? With shoulders squared, chin tucked in, I said, "May I see Mr. Peterson's care plan?"

I was met with a flutter of eyelids. "And you are?"

"Oh, sorry, of course, I'm his daughter." Rewording my request, I offered, "Seeing his list of medications would be a helpful start." I smiled and concentrated on steady eye contact.

"Certainly."

The list was short, but one entry glared at me like high-beam headlights. "Why is he getting heart medication? He has never been diagnosed with heart trouble." Without a word, with no explanation, the medication was removed. Wariness struck. My eyes saw deeper, clearer. A new resolve stiffened my spine. Did the nurse look shorter?

Had I not continued to oversee what medications he was prescribed, I would have missed the heart medication reappearing in his care plan. Did some kind of policy or "standard operating procedure" drive directions to staff? Constant vigilance became my mantra.

Dad raised another care issue when he complained that his mouth was sore. I looked in his mouth. Dad had always taken care of himself. I felt awkward and invasive asking him to open his mouth as I peered in. I lifted his lips to expose red and swollen gums. Furious that Dad was not getting good mouth care, I demanded that the nursing staff provide what had been promised and what we paid for, or I would deduct the fee from the facility's charges. Neither my ire nor my threat fazed them. Dad's teeth were not taken care of. I felt that the only way I would know his teeth were brushed was to do it myself.

But what about the other patients? If my dad was treated that way—who was watching out for the others? We managed to get Dad through without any further mishaps. The staff was alerted that we were watching. Yet suffering was all around. Again my human limitations overwhelmed me and fed my guilt for not doing enough.

For Dad's sake, my first responsibility, I had to overcome the darkness of such a place by offering a comforting presence. He continued to surprise me with his occasional lucid moments.

Once, I was sitting in the dining with him while Mother wheeled others to the table, adjusted their bibs, and poured coffee. Dad turned to me, concern furrowing his brow. "Look at her helping everyone. Who's going to take care of her when I'm gone?"

I bowed my head and paused, bathing in his grace. I took his hand. "I will, Dad. I will," I said. In another lucid moment, Mother and I were sitting on his bed as he relaxed in his lounge chair. He turned to us, his face beaming, and said, "This is an afternoon I will never forget, being with the most important people in the world, you two." Then he sang, "I can't give you anything, but love, baby." Mother and I harmonized. On the last note his arms expanded in a midair embrace. For a brief moment we were the three bears again.

Over the remaining months of his life, the answer to my desperate prayer came to me through the experience of just being there for both Mother and Dad. The answer was that there is suffering and that suffering can be a gift. When Dad could no longer walk, when he could no longer feed himself or remember what he had to eat moments before, when his life was distilled to his very spirit, one thing remained: Love. Love was all he had to give, and love was all he could receive. The greatest gift of all, and it was all we had.

He demonstrated that love once again the week before he died. The nursing assistant wheeled him outside. "Are you comfortable, Mr. Peterson?"

He responded, "Yes, I am. And are you all right?"

For four years he showed us how to live as he suffered and how to live as he died, a great spirit within an ordinary man.

On his last night, I stood at the foot of his bed. He was still, his mouth open to catch the breath that did not come. His arms, which had once held me and the face that had smiled at me were no longer important. His great spirit had left. He had found a space to slip through, escaping the brain-numbed loss of a wife's face, the confusion of scooping up food from his plate and dumping it in his coffee, the lost connectedness of opening his mouth when he was asked to close his eyes.

The mortician removed his body from the room. Mother went to the closet and pulled out his favorite blue sweater, his red socks. "Would you like these?" she asked me, holding them out to me. His scent lingered, comforting me with his presence. As naturally as anything I have ever done, I reached for the sweater and socks. I slipped on the sweater and sat in his chair while I pulled on his red socks, remnant of an embrace, but an embrace just the same. A daughter had learned her lesson, and a dad had completed his work.

Something Good

Elisa Jay

Shaking her purse, my mother emptied the last of its contents onto a pillow. "Ah! Here it is!" she said, holding up a small box of chocolates. "Caramel. The *best*," she smiled, inhaling, as I carried two cups of tea to the table. Leaning over her seat, she smiled at the Shih Tzu looking up at her expectantly. "But not for you, Gigi. Never chocolate for you." We laughed and settled into ourselves, turning on the T.V.

It had become our favorite ritual: Tea. Sweet treats. The Food Network blaring in the background. During commercial breaks we caught up on everything from celebrities to politics. And inevitably, we'd discuss the current events surrounding Dad's condition: The hospital visits, the doctors, nurses. I'd share a theory about his salt intake being more serious than sugar. Mom would lament the expense of medications. And always, we'd vent our frustrations: The constant feeling of loss, the misunderstandings of well-meaning loved ones, how badly our own muscles ached.

But these were good moments, stolen while Dad was at the adult day care center or sleeping peacefully in his room, and the stars aligned so that both my mother and I were free. We seized these opportunities to spend time with the only other person who understood what we were feeling - each other.

Within the context of caregiving we were fortunate. Having each other allowed us wider respite. We took turns sleeping on the couch, cleaning, and cultivating patience. The weight of everything that needed doing was distributed between us. But despite this advantage, we suffered, until we came to understand what we had. Often, like when we watched Dad's Parkinson's rob him of basic functions, we didn't realize what to appreciate until it was lost. And we had lost many things including money, time, acquaintances, and sleep. We became overwhelmed, plagued by a constant sense that we were drowning.

Spending my twenties caregiving had increasingly made me angry. Dad had been diagnosed during my last semester of college, and caring for him after graduating had initially been an optimistic and facile decision. But I hadn't appreciated how quickly his condition would change him or that he wasn't going to improve. Later, when we calculated the cost of a part-time caregiver and realized we couldn't afford it, my spirits really sank. My mother, whose work provided the health insurance we relied on, could not give up her position. To make matters worse, we were bombarded with irritating questions and opinions from onlookers. What were my plans and goals, outside of *this*? Would I return to school to study something more useful than literature? Had my mother considered going entirely organic for her husband's diet? Had we considered praying more? These intrusive queries were antagonizing to say the least in light of our daily difficulties. Carrying adult diapers from the bathroom while focusing on my failures as an educated adult began to make me feel bitter. So did appearing to be a parasite instead of my parents' helpmate in the eyes of others.

Years passed like that until slowly change bloomed. I gradually began to notice how strikingly good I felt when simple pleasures appeared. I relished the difference a good night's sleep made. Little things caught my eye: An especially sweet nectarine. Charming postage stamps or a smooth pen provided tinges of delight. A trip to a high-end spice shop yielded the discovery of delicious, salt-free spice blends. "You don't even notice the absence of salt, when the spices are good quality!" the attendant glowed. Equally rewarding was watching Dad smack his lips appreciatively when he tasted the spices.

I also began to notice that I was never angry when I drank tea, so I began to revel in the ritual of brewing each cup. I shared my newfound tea pleasure with my mother, and we developed a fondness for drinking tea in bed, when Dad was tucked in. Then desserts began to appear. A vintage tray table, gifted to us from my late grandmother, found its way to regular use.

We began to talk more honestly. As two consummate people-pleasers, it was a profound relief when we confessed the many ways in which we felt injured when people said silly things. The more we released these suppressed feelings, the more we began to feel grateful for the family and friends who were genuine comforts. We also noticed any positive improvement in dad's condition and celebrated each small victory. Above all, we relished our girl talk and the luxury of being ourselves. Our sense of humanity was somehow restored.

Caregiving is like being caught in a riptide. The current pulls its captive in deeper, sometimes slamming it against the ocean floor. It's urgent to swim for safety, to return to land, but often that means moving in tiring directions to avoid going under. The way to safety can be circuitous.

Our little tea parties did not stop Dad's challenging condition, but they did help keep us afloat during an arduous journey that continued to twist and turn. Still, a quiet moment, an indulgent treat, a thing of beauty helped us remain mindful of the good things in life. And for that, we are ever grateful.

Steering Through the Fog

Nancy Smiler Levinson

When my husband, Irwin, a physician and a gentle, beautiful man, was diagnosed with Alzheimer's Disease, he slid into a protective cocoon, remaining in denial until his memory had so declined that it was impossible for him to comprehend anything. With the first mention of memory loss to him, encouraging his seeking a physical exam to rule out any other illness that might be responsible, he refused. He simply insisted, during those years in his late seventies, that forgetting a name or movie title was "age appropriate."

He would snap at me and our two sons defensively, "You never went to medical school, so what makes you think you know about diseases?" He always had an answer that satisfied his need. The three of us came to understand that need, and we finally accepted the futility of trying to rationalize with irrationality.

Acceptance is a key word for caregivers, family, and friends— then a new acceptance for each new faltering stage of the patient's disease. And although it's not always easy, keeping family members together in mind and action is also vital in caring for a patient, as well as for helping each other to take care of themselves. A constant support group cry to caregivers is, "Take care of yourself, too!"

My sons, Matt and Dan, and I formed a "team," deciding that major decisions must be agreed upon, no matter what compromises or back-downs were needed. During our agreement, light-heartedly, Matt added one last rule: "No eye-rolling in front of Dad."

As primary caregiver, I was fortunate as well that both guys were there for me and their dad, visiting, working large-piece jigsaw puzzles with him, taking him out to play miniature golf, and giving me time for myself. One evening I joined them at Dodger Stadium, where I held Irwin's hand to comfort him in an unfamiliar venue and to keep him from getting lost in the crowd.

Early on, our "team" acknowledged that taking the car away would be tearing away a symbol of control and a means of independence. Irwin was still driving in the neighborhood. When I mentioned his *not* driving, he replied with clenched teeth, "Don't go down that path." State law obligates a physician to contact the DMV when suspicious of a patient's state of mind and ability to drive safely. We three agreed to ask the doctor to write a letter. At the same time I tried letting go of guilt when talking behind my husband's back.

During the license removal process, one evening Irwin and I decided to have dinner in a neighborhood restaurant. "Hey— why don't I drive," I said.

"What *are* you talking about?" Irwin answered.

"It's a good idea," I said, trying to sound casual with my suggested strategy. "You always drive me. Now I'll drive you."

"Haven't I always been a safe driver?" he answered.

That was true. But I could not yield. "It's just not a good idea for you to drive, darling," I said even-toned, returning to the kitchen to cobble a supper together.

In the doctor's office Irwin continued to reject everything the doctor said regarding *not* driving. He scorned every suggestion, especially taking a driver's evaluation program which would have given him a direct written report. In his mind "evaluation" meant "instruction."

"No thank you," he said. "I know how to drive. My skills are good. In fact, I'm better than most at my age."

After that I tried a foolish trick, hiding the car keys. As expected, that blew up out of proportion, and I grew increasingly anxious waited for the DMV notice. Suddenly, one afternoon Irwin said he was going to the mall nearby and drove off. Unable to stop him, I paced, deeply worried. What if…what if… Then the phone rang. I grabbed the receiver. "Will you accept a collect call?" the operator asked. (I'll never know how he managed to find a pay phone in 2006.) Irwin had lost his car. I hurried to get him, meeting at a spot I was sure he would find and remain — the bakery department of the market.

With him in my passenger seat I slowly drove every aisle of the parking structure, back and forth on all levels, then returned to the first level. Finally, we found the car, one hour and ten minutes later. Irwin didn't see this as peculiar. I knew he'd have forgotten the incident an hour later, denying that it happened. I had to let it go.

Finally, the long-awaited Department of Motor Vehicles letter arrived. I handed it to Irwin while I breathed deeply. The letter stated their decision clearly: *Your license is revoked, as of January 1, 2007. However, should you choose to contest the directive you are offered to set an appointment for a hearing.*" He blanched, scowling at me. "Are *you* behind this?" Seeing a box with an X by the word "dementia," he ranted. "Who says I am demented! This is unacceptable. A mistake. Who turned me in?"

There was nothing left for me to say. To complicate matters, I couldn't sort out my own muddled feelings which included profound sadness and utter helplessness.

Believing he was invited to retake an exam, Irwin managed to send for a revised, expanded driver's manual. He made a date at a DMV office but forgot the date or lost the scratch papers of jotted notes. So he continued to "study" the manual. He asked me to vow not to tell a soul about this driver's license "mistake." Our sons spoke directly to him. "Why don't you let the driver's license go, Dad? It's the responsible thing to do." Later he told me, "Those guys don't know what they're talking about."

Day after day Irwin opened the manual, often not knowing the reason he held it in his hand. But in his determination to drive he steered forward into a tempest that left him without direction. Then the hearing date arrived. He changed shirts, ties, and sweaters several times in order to appear a fine, well-dressed gentleman. In the car, as I drove, he looked at the morning newspaper. It's Wednesday, January 31," he recited over and over. "The president is George Bush." Then Irwin asked that I "review why we are in Iraq." Next he said, "Explain the difference between the Shia and the Sunnis." My eyes hugged the road, hands gripping the wheel, foot steady on the accelerator. What was holding me together as profound heartache and pity crushed my heart?

At the DMV office a woman sat opposite him at a large desk. She directed me to a folding chair against a wall, forbidding me to speak. Then she turned on a tape recorder and verified Irwin's name, address and license number. Then she handed him the doctor's letter, which indicated "mild, cognitive impairment."

He registered shock, vehemently denying the accusation. Soon tempered, he reviewed his perfect driving record, adding that he read three newspapers a day and was a good citizen. With further questioning, he became repetitious, revealing his confusion and giving himself away. I sat still while my heart shattered into kaleidoscopic pieces.

By the time we reached home, Irwin believed that his renewed license would arrive by mail. Instead, within days, he received a definitive letter of license revocation.

Our rough journey continued as I became the lone, legal driver and he morphed into my constant adviser. "Move over to the right lane! Watch out! There's a lady crossing the street. You're exceeding the speed limit. Who taught you how to parallel park? You're too close to the curb!"

Sometimes I snapped back. But mostly I swallowed hard and yet again began to accept this new phase of dementia. Then I continued navigating our jarring journey.

The Meaning of Care

T.M. Bradshaw

At a retreat weekend, a new friend comments, "Your husband needs quite a bit of care, doesn't he?" I am taken aback. Certainly there are things he can no longer do because of his Parkinson's, like driving, but I view the things I do for him more as little favors than care in a dance of mutual support.

If he needs to go to the library on chess club day, I drop him off. I go along on doctors' appointments—usually one every two months, but some months it's as many as four visits. I am his second set of ears. I adjust his suspenders when he gets them tangled up. I fill his daily and weekly pill organizers to be sure the right pills are in the right places. I cook because I always have, but now I wash dishes, too, because he just hasn't gotten around to them. I inspect cutlery that are theoretically clean, because his vision doesn't reveal dried-on spaghetti sauce or because loss of muscle tone doesn't allow for vigorous scrubbing. I rearrange laundry hung outdoors, because spatial reality is fluid for him, and I don't like to see pants pinned to the sagging clothesline lying on the ground while socks fly freely from their higher position. I play cards and Scrabble, because games are good for him, even when I have more pressing tasks I'd rather be doing.

But none of this seems like care, because to me, "care" generates visions of spoon-feeding, sponge baths, and diaper changing.

Now my new friend's comment has made me reassess the situation. I realize how much has changed since my husband's diagnosis five earlier. The losses he has suffered have crept up on us, so that it's hard to see the overall impact. It's like gaining a pound or two a year—after a number of years the change in weight and appearance is a jolt.

Her offhand remark sent me to the dictionary to consider the various meanings of "care." I see that as a verb it means "to have affection for." Certainly that's true; he is my husband. "To mind; to be concerned." Again, true because it bothers me to see the things he is no longer able to do. Sometimes those things also bother me because they encroach on my space and plans. My life is circumscribed by his losses, too. "To have, feel, or exercise care." Ah, yes, the endless battle to be patient and gentle, to overcome frustration with things that he cannot help and that he too finds frustrating.

As a noun the word means "mental suffering; grief." There are times when watching him struggle brings me to tears, always for him, never me. "A burdensome sense of responsibility." While he is not a burden, there is a real and sometimes frightening sense of that responsibility. Unlike with a child, when we know what we're signing up for, in marriage we expect a partnership that includes shared burdens. It may not always be fifty-fifty, in fact it rarely is, but sharing burdens is expected. Instead, household scheduling, bill-paying, and acting as liaison to insurance companies or doctors' offices lands squarely on my shoulders now. "Painstaking or watchful attention; heed; caution." Stairs and uneven surfaces require extra attention. Ensuring that regular paths are obstacle-free and that things are put back where they belong requires paying attention. The situation calls for a streamlined life but not a rearranged one.

In the retirement I had pictured, both of us appeared active and healthy, eagerly following our own interests. The imagined days started with pleasant conversation at breakfast, each detailing individual agendas, and finishing dinner with tales of how the day had unfolded. But spending most of the day together means missing out on two individual views of the world. It's another small loss for both of us.

Did my new friend comment on how much care my husband needs because what she observed tends to be things one sees in public? Does she realize that Parkinson's Disease is more than a tremor that affects many parts of the body? Visual problems are a good example: Since all muscles are weakened, or brain signals to muscles are compromised, focus isn't always immediate. Interpreting what the eyes see is also compromised. Add a hallucination or two, and sight cannot be trusted. Balance and gait are affected, so I hold my husband's hand, appearing to lead him, in unfamiliar places. I fill his plate in a buffet line, or I carry his plate to our table. People with Parkinson's often "freeze," unable to take the next step. When that happens, I help him resume motion with a gentle push, or I point to the spot on the floor where his foot should go next. Sadly, the problems that matter least in terms being oneself are the most visible ones to others. They are what lead to perceptions of disability and feeble-mindedness.

And that's where a different kind of care takes over, because I care deeply that others see past these surface issues so that they can really know the man my husband still is. That would be good for him. For them, it would be an enlightening experience.

A Good Day

Caroline Johnson

He was having a good day. A nurse evaluated him. He couldn't answer most questions, but he knew it was spring. He couldn't sign his name. He thought it was January. Still, he was having a good day.

I wanted to leave. I had done my time—spent hours with the nurse and his caregiver. I had to grade papers, buy some groceries, get home to have dinner with my husband. But he was having a good day, and when I tried to say good-bye, he asked me when he would see me again. I told him soon, and that I would bring cake.

"Cake?" he asked, expectantly. I asked him what kind he would like. "Chocolate," he said from his hospital bed.

So I left and went to Jewel, then returned with two giant pieces of cake. Red velvet with cream cheese frosting, and marble cake frosted with chocolate. He chose the red velvet.

I spooned fed the red velvet cake into his mouth. He said it was very good. Afterwards, I turned on CNN and stayed to chat. He played with my key chain like an infant. He reached up and tried to unzip my sweatshirt. He pointed to my T-shirt.

"It's the Scream," I said. "A painting by Edvard Munch."

He smiled and reached out to touch me. He said one word.

"What did you say, Dad?" I asked.

"Heart," he whispered, then closed his eyes.

Hospice

Caroline Johnson

When you watch someone die
you must sit up close and open
your heart to pronounce each vowel,
you must let your loved one
embrace the air, let his arm
extend towards infinity,
you must help him
touch the stars.

When you watch your father die
remember it is a privilege
to stroke his stone cheek,
to kiss his forehead,
to tuck his hair behind his ears.
You must try not to be
so important, you must wave
when he decides to leave.

When you watch a bomber pilot die
who once got lost in the threshold
of a dream, remember he no longer
needs his walker, his cane, his wheelchair
remember there will come a day
when he will no longer need you
will no longer need his body
though you will pray for him

to bring back the light as he flies
past 1,000 sunrises in the sky.

The Caregiver[2]

Caroline Johnson

See this Lithuanian woman. She has been
feeding my father dinners of mashed turkey
and broccoli, potato pancakes, washing his
clothes, bathing him, offering him the choice
between Wolf Blitzer and Vanna White for years.

Observe her hands as they gently push his body
to the side of the hospital bed. They are covered
with latex gloves. Consider the way she has taught
me to tenderly pull up his socks and cover him
with a quilt, put drops in his eyes, rub powder
on a rash, splash his neck with Old Spice, then
bend down to kiss his cheek goodnight.

You must come closer, you must hang up your jacket,
be prepared to spend hours listening to his slurred
speech, help feed him applesauce with vitamins,
raise and lower his bed, monitor his erratic heartbeat.
Remember what he has given up—his Buick LeSabre,
his cane, his walker, then finally his wheelchair, to get
to where he now lives--a bed with guard rails.

Go to the night-stand and offer him a Frango Mint,
put on his favorite Garrison Keillor CD. Listen as he
smiles with his one good eye and whispers something
so faint, you ask him to repeat, "I'm lucky."
Think about all this while driving the long way home.

[2] First appeared in Lunch Ticket, January 2016. Reprinted by permission of the author.

You may get angry at the world, like I do, until you get home
and see your husband asleep in the Lazy- Boy, bare
legs dangling. Until you suddenly realize what the caregiver
has taught you as, without a word, you slowly rub lotion
onto your husband's chapped heels, then cover his ice-cold feet.

PART THREE

Saying Goodbye

My Voyage to the Edge

Susan Leader

My mother was very particular about her coiffure, rarely permitting me to touch her perfect natural curls, much less brush or comb them. This prerogative she preserved through all her years as a farmer and mother of three to her very last, as a semi-invalid. Imagine my shock, then, when a comb was placed firmly between my fingers with instructions to arrange the beloved locks anyway I pleased.

"Miriam's hair is still beautiful," the head priestess whispered in my ear as she strode briskly around the chilled room passing out disposable gloves.

My mother's hair was the last remaining identifiable feature of her now inert body. Trapped in a macabre game of 'Corpse-Hairdressing Barbie," I ran an oddly ordinary comb through dense white curls, gingerly lifting the swollen head with one hand to reach the tangled mat underneath. Then, with my pinky, I twisted my mother's bangs into a pair of quotation marks right in the center of her forehead, the way she used to do for me.

* * * * *

In the thirty-nine hours since she died, my mother's petite ninety-two-and-one-half-year-old body has filled with fluid, inflating into the grotesque Venus de Willendorf laid out before me on a long white plastic table in the bowels of the funeral home. A rubber hose dangles snake-like nearby, screwed into the warm water tap of an ancient porcelain sink. Gathering silently around it, we five women pour clear water over our palms from a ceremonial two-handled cup, three times in a row.

Miriam died on the Festival of Sukkot, described in Ecclesiastes as 'A time to plant and a time to pluck up that which has been planted'. This year the festival ran into Shabbat (the Sabbath) as well. Therefore, in accordance with traditional Jewish protocol, burial could not occur until Sunday. So we tucked my mother's body into her bed at home, in a little room off the kitchen, where, despite emitting the sharp scent of decomposing flesh, it remained at the center of family life over the course of one last weekend.

My mother barely made ends meet in life. Yet, despite her inconsistent relationship with establishment Judaism, she had prepaid the one hundred percent complete traditional treatment after death, thus sending my secular family down a surprising path of discovery. From *shemira*, guarding the body until burial, to sitting *shiva* afterwards, the therapeutic nature of Jewish rituals surrounding death supported us. In every instance, not only did we the survivors take care; we were cared for royally in return. Surely this had been my mother's intention: her last, and lasting, gift to us.

I had always imagined the custom of *taharah*, the washing of the body, to be an arcane enterprise reserved for the ultra-orthodox, or the merely brave within whose ranks I did not count myself. What on earth had possessed my mother to budget over six thousand dollars for all this nonsense? Hadn't my father, who predeceased her, always said, "Just put me on the compost pile." Accordingly, we had spread his cremains in the woods in Vermont decades ago, with hardly a marker.

My understanding of *tahara* shifted when I dropped by the funeral home on my way downtown to grab a snack before my mother's funeral service. Providentially, four priestesses, members of the local *chevra kaddisha*, or Jewish burial society, reached out from the dim lobby where they were assembling and drew me into their ranks. One of them, an old friend of my mother's, motioned me towards a narrow opening in the wall. Exposed pipes clearly indicated the working parts of the establishment. I had literally one minute to overcome my fear of death. Abandoning my plans for a soy latte and sushi to go, I followed the group in its descent to the basement.

Transported into a different dimension, I was suddenly part of an esoteric sisterhood, chanting age-old *taharah* prayers begging Miriam's forgiveness for any indignity inadvertently inflicted upon her body as we fulfilled the sacred duty to wash it.

Despite our painstaking care, my mother's now purple colored skin peeled off her body in cobweb-like tatters as ten infinitely gentle hands dabbed at it from all sides with fine washcloths. I felt dizzy, gagged by the smell of decaying meat, drowning in dank fluid. The distorted misshapen mass laid out before me had been my beautiful mother Miriam, Sister of Moses, the archetypal water witch. Even in death she still gathered her waters, commanding them to rise.

The veteran team of priestesses had taken a big risk by including me in their rites.

Parroting everything they said and did, I did not allow myself conscious thought. By this means I managed not to scream, faint, run away or otherwise betray their trust. My reward was safe passage to the edge. In little more than an hour, I grew from a squeamish, superstitious child to an empowered adult able to stare down Death, at least temporarily, while in the company of these wise women!

We made rapid progress with the washing. As with most women's work, many hands made it light. My mind's eye flashed on a young Miriam, attired in folkloric peasant blouse and long flowing skirt, hanging laundry to dry in the wind on a mountainside near Pikes Falls, Vermont, in 1949 with a group of her friends.

Recognizing the impossibility of turning the soggy decomposing body over, we settled for prayerfully levitating it off the table for a split second. It was clear: no more could be done, without doing harm.

Our leader, Cleo, anticipating the next step, took me aside to demonstrate how to tie the gossamer thin drawstrings which would secure Miriam's white burial garments pants, head shroud and shirtsleeves, in the complicated triple-fingered design of a *shaddai*, the Hebrew letter *shin* signifying God's name. Shaken by the utter finality of the fitting of the head shroud, the climactic moment for me of this *taharah* ritual, I had to rip off my clumsy protective gloves before finally succeeding in tying a reasonable *shaddai* around my mother's neck, pointing downwards towards her heart. A Ziplock bag filled with soil from the Holy Land was thrust into my hand. Kind hands guided me in pouring out a small hill of it onto a tray. I deposited it barehanded into a corner of the plain pine coffin. It was the same dirt my mother collected between her toes as a young *kibbutznik*, tending her beloved fields of carrots.

As an extra offering, I also placed in the coffin the accursed oversized toenail cutting shears, with all the memories they invoked of my sister and me, assisted by a parade of visiting nurses, struggling to keep my mother's horny misshapen toenails in check through her last declining years.

The women of the *chevra kadisha*, literally "sacred society," considered a trip to the *mikveh* (ritual bath) after our task was complete. Disappointingly, not enough time remained for us to ritually bathe ourselves before the funeral service was scheduled to begin.

I returned home the following day to discover a small well in the woods behind my house which had been completely dry all summer had miraculously filled to its brim. I immersed myself symbolically in the cool water.

Unbelievably, an old friend called that same evening to ask me, a potter, if I would be willing to help him create a cremation urn for his son, who had just been found dead of an overdose.

Fortified by my experience with the women of the *chevra kadisha*, I heard myself saying yes, please come to my house. Together we should be able to do this. And we did.

Winter Hours

Tzivia Gover

When I visit my mother these days, I often leave with something of hers in my overnight bag: a t-shirt, a pair of socks, a book.

I'm just taking what she would have given. She used to, when she was in her right mind, tell me to keep anything I'd borrowed while I was visiting—a scarf, a pair of sandals—or she would buy me little gifts as we walked through her neighborhood in New York. But now she is not in her right mind, and our old routines are fading, just as the glint in her green eyes is slipping into a milky half-asleep stare.

It used to be that from time to time, I'd receive in the mail a package from her. I'd slip open the mailer, then unwrap layers of pastel-colored tissue paper to find a slim volume of poetry by one of our favorite poets. Now, she doesn't mail things. She sounds out words painstakingly, and with a certain effortful pride, as I did when I was learning to read as a small child and she was encouraging me.

So on a recent visit I pulled the book *Winter Hours* by Mary Oliver from a shelf in her study. I was attracted to the slender book with the green and blue cover; just like one I might have received in the mail from her. I slipped it into my bag, knowing she'd never miss it.

Later I realized I was so taken by the beach-glass hues of the cover, and the delicately drawn sailboat bisecting its horizon, that I missed the somber weight of the title: Winter Hours. And so, when I began to read it, I was surprised by how serious the volume was.

That visit when I took the book coincided with the time when my mother's condition took a turn for the worse. Her sweet, childlike senility had devolved into a depressed, angry fog. Whereas before she had forgotten words, names, and past events—now she was forgetting the function of ordinary objects. She'd lift a lipstick and say, "I can't remember what I do with this."

The slipping away started slowly. At first she'd ask me when I was coming to visit. Then she'd ask the same question again. And again. She'd call me, and ten minutes after we hung up she'd call back, oblivious of this eerie repetition.

The doctors first referred to her condition as "normal age-related memory loss," then "Temporal Lobe Dementia." And recently her neurologist used the word Alzheimer's.

She's 79, and I'm 50. Suddenly I'm sensing a darkness in the world I'd never noticed before. Mortality—mine and hers—is now undeniable. My gray hairs. Her daily losses. My friends' gathering diagnoses. My mother no longer knows the word for daughter.

At first, when I started to feel the sadness of all these changes, I considered taking anti-depressants. But I decided to try and buoy my mood with a regimen of meditation and self-help books, instead. And meanwhile, over breakfast each morning, I'd read a few pages of Oliver's book.

I teach poetry to teens for a living, and yet I'd been feeling disconnected from it; couldn't quite justify to myself, let alone my resistant students, why poems mattered.

Oliver reminded me.

She wrote of Robert Frost's inner darkness; his grim outlook carried on the cheerful cadences of his diction. She wrote of Whitman's loneliness, and Hopkins' slides into sorrow and his ecstatic flights of joy.

The steady pace of Oliver's words, well placed, elegant, and unhurried—gave me solace. So, too, did the full spectrum of the poets' emotions, from bliss to despair, and their ability to sculpt beauty and meaning from life's shadowy passages.

Gradually, I felt myself relaxing into my sorrow. I stopped calling it depression, instead naming it *feeling*: Feeling the grief of my mother's decline and of the end of my own youth. The acceptance that life is about letting go; that despite my chronically upbeat insistence on affirmation and self-growth, we are all spinning unceasingly toward death—and worse—suffering lurks in the corners, ready to pounce.

During those literary interludes at the breakfast table I was hammocked in the delight of words stretching toward stark and beautiful truth. I was comforted by the saying of the bare fact of it; of storms, of death, of plummeting moods that also rose to divine heights.

One morning as I read, my fingertips hit a thin obstacle, something stuck to the inside back cover. I flipped the pages to find a small envelope taped to it. Inside was a note card decorated with holly leaves and berries. It was from one of my mother's many boyfriends, wishing her a "Merry Christmas or Happy Solstice" (offering her the choice, she being a non-religious Jew). He wrote that with this book, the one now in my hands, he was introducing her to one of his "friends" after she had introduced him to so many of hers.

This glimpse into my mother's private love life burst through my morning reading like sun streaming through the kitchen window. My mother was both secret and prideful about her liaisons with men. She liked people to know she had lovers, but I only found out particulars when I stumbled upon them. I remembered coming across this man in her living room: wiry, bespectacled, and on at least one occasion, accompanied by a big, sloppy black dog. Now I tried to imagine what poets she had introduced him to. I saw him at last as a worthy suitor, one who knew something of my mother that was worth knowing.

Had my mother ever read this book? Fourteen years after it was published, the book had a brand new crispness to it. There was no evidence that she had opened it, save to un-stick the envelope at the back, and tuck it back away. No passage was underlined; no notes were jotted in the margins. No page was turned down at the corner. Only now, there was the occasional smudge of tea from where I'd rested my mug while I read, and a few post-it notes I placed on pages to mark favorite phrases.

But the gifts I was receiving from reading it—unexpected and unlikely pockets of comfort—seemed to be for both of us.

As I drew closer to the end, I read more slowly. And when I got to the final page, I couldn't help myself. I cried. I cried because my mother was still giving me gifts, even when she could no longer know it. And I cried because here it was, this book, ending.

A Hymn to Love

Sloane Dawson

It was a struggle, but with a good push of the wheelchair, I made it through the doors into the reception area. We were a little late. The six women waiting for us looked questioningly at me, then smiled as they came towards us to tie colorful balloons to the wheelchair. Did they know it was my mother's 98th birthday, or were balloons a welcome gesture for all new residents?

I was so upset at the thought of incarcerating my beloved mother in a nursing home, and on her birthday that I ignored the balloons and the women. Looking at my mother's sweet face, I saw a happy countenance and a winning smile as she responded positively to all the attention, so typical of her gentle disposition. One of the women said, "My! Your mother is so young looking." This was a common observation I'd become used to. I'd heard it many times when growing up.

At 98, Mother still had a full head of beautiful brown hair and her tight skin remained unblemished. Even at 98 she had no liver spots or moles, probably because of her aversion to the sun, coupled with good genes. She took no medicine and never had. The need for a wheelchair was due to knees that had simply worn out and could no longer support her light frame.

"Come," the woman who had introduced herself as Anna, said. "I'll show you your room."

As we proceeded slowly down a long hall like newly arrived guests at a somber social event, we were scrutinized by other residents sitting along the walls on benches or in wheelchairs.

Mother looked at everyone and everything with great interest and curiosity. Reaching out to some of the people we passed, she smiled sweetly and with compassion, patting their arms, saying hello, or waving.

These good signs comforted me somewhat, as did visiting the hairdresser, where I opened an account for Mother and made an appointment for a cut and perm. Things were going well, I thought, keeping my anxiety at bay. I stayed until dinnertime, when I hugged her goodbye, promising I'd be back the next day.

After a sleepless night riddled with guilt and remorse, I told myself that if she was unhappy or I didn't like the situation, I would bring her home. She did come home for the day a month later to celebrate her birthday, belatedly, with family. By that time she did not know her grandson and had forgotten living in her home. At that point I knew she had made the transition and that keeping her in the nursing home was not only safe but the best thing for her welfare, as her dementia slowly diminished her once active mind.

The nursing home was still amazed by her young appearance. When I asked why she hadn't had the promised permanent the reply was, "We don't perm dyed hair." I laughed. "That's her natural hair color. She has never dyed her hair or used any cosmetics except lipstick!" She quickly got her perm.

For the next three years, I went every day to see Mother. She often sat in the window watching for me to arrive as she leafed through magazines the receptionist provided. They sometimes discussed the pictures, laughing and chatting together. I was grateful for this kind young woman, who over the years loved and watched out for my mother when I wasn't with her.

On one occasion when I arrived, I couldn't find Mother. She wasn't at the window or in her room. Panicked, I raced up and down the halls inquiring about her. Then I passed a resident's room, and there she was, sitting next to the bed holding a very ill woman's hand and singing softly to her. In her own dementia,

Mother still had the same kind, caring soul that she'd always had, and now she was still sharing and comforting others.

I thought back to the incidents that had prompted my decision to put her in the nursing home: Finding a sandwich hidden in the pots and pans cupboard, pouring the contents of her potty chair on the floor. These were only a few of the incidents that made me liken my job as caretaker to that of a mother with a two-year-old child who required constant attention. I did this monitoring willingly and without rancor or regret; I loved my mother dearly and appreciated the care she had given me as a child. She not only gave my brother and me life; she had kept us alive by nursing us through many serious childhood illnesses. She never complained and always gave us tender, devoted care. So it was payback time for me, and I gladly reciprocated with the same patience and kindness.

Before Mother entered the nursing home, I slept very little, always ready to pounce from my bed as I heard her get up to use the bathroom. Assuring myself that she was safely back in bed, I dozed lightly.

One night I heard unusual thumping and rushed into her room to find her sitting up in bed, arms waving wildly, her body banging against the wall. I immediately hit the life-line button she wore on her wrist and urged an ambulance to take her to the hospital. It was two in the morning. Groggy and lacking sleep, I followed in my car, hoping desperately that she would be okay. She was. Everything checked out fine. As usual, she had the blood pressure of a child, and her heart was normal. She had possibly suffered a small stroke and had a seizure.

A few more of these episodes ensued. When one occurred, I held her in my arms and rocked her gently until it ended. Only a few minutes in duration, these occasions frightened me terribly, while Mother seemed unaware that they had occurred. These seizures marked the start of Mother's mental deterioration. No longer able to carry on a conversation, she spoke in clipped, sometimes incoherent sentences.

One night as I slept lightly, I startled. Something was not right. I raced towards her room. She was not there or in the bathroom. Then I noticed all the lights were on. I went to the kitchen, and there she was, sitting at the table, smiling and asking me where breakfast was. It was three o'clock in the morning.

About this time Mother started falling out of bed during the night. I would rush to her aid, checking to see if she was hurt. With her clinging to me and pushing herself up, I was able to lift her back on to the bed. One night, I heard the now familiar thump and rushed to her side. I tried to get her back into bed, but she couldn't help me. We struggled together until my strength gave out, silent tears welling up in my eyes. I decided to take the mattress off the bed and put it on the floor, where I could then roll her on to it. Covering her, I placed her head gently on her pillow. It was shortly after three in the morning. Whom could I call to help? I lay down on the box spring next to her and held her hand until she slept, and we spent the rest of the night lying there together, with me watching her, so she wouldn't be frightened if she awoke on her floor bed. At 7:30 in the morning I phoned the young man who did our yard work. He lived nearby and was on the rescue squad. He arrived immediately, his strong six-foot frame lifting her like a feather and depositing her in her wheelchair while we reassembled the bed.

"You could have called me in the night," he said. "I would have come right over." His words were comforting and helped me feel less alone.

After several more traumatic events occurred, we found ourselves at the nursing home, me a day resident looking after their permanent charge. I helped in the activities room, sitting with Mother and other residents, often doing simple arts and crafts or playing games. Mother and I also attended parties and other events in her new home, and she appeared to be comfortable and happy.

Every Sunday a non-denominational church service was held. We went to them too, sitting side-by-side, holding hands as the pastor spoke. When sheets of paper with hymns printed on them were handed out, Mother set hers aside until the piano music started. Then she sang in a steady sweet voice, remembering all the words to verses she hadn't heard in over sixty years. Tears filled my eyes. I was amazed that she could do this despite the fact that she now barely spoke.

One Sunday, Mother looked at me and squeezed my hand, struggling to speak. I waited, smiling encouragement. I saw the enormous effort it was taking and sensed her determination. Finally, with halting words, she said, "Thank you for loving me so much and taking such good care of me." I hugged her to me, tears flowing.

They still haven't stopped. But now that she is gone, I weep, knowing that sometimes love is enough. I understand that relinquishing physical caretaking doesn't mean relinquishing loving care. It's okay to seek help, because at the end of the day, you are always the primary caregiver, the only one who can offer the power of love as life fades ever so slowly away.

Watching[3]

Susan Cushman

"I hope it's soon." Her voice is calm, with a touch of weariness.

I stumble over the Greek phrase that means "God willing." She nods and smiles at my effort.

We're sitting in a tiny study which opens onto the balcony at my friend's retirement home in a Memphis suburb. It's a corner apartment, facing southwest. An hour ago the view from the balcony was cinematic. The sun's late afternoon rays had been diffused by a gathering of milky clouds, slightly backlit, leaving an artist's dream sky in its setting wake. Just when I thought it was gone, it made a brief encore appearance at the horizon — more intense than its hazy afternoon showing. Now I look at my friend and wonder if her departure will follow this pattern.

Urania is eighty-six. She has end stage metastatic bone cancer. I'm spending a few days with her between her children's shifts, which have increased in frequency and duration over the past few weeks. Her daughters live in New York City, and my mother lives in Mississippi, so Urania and I sort of adopted each other a few years back. I'm not the only one who considers her their unofficial "yia yia." She takes everyone in, regardless of race, religion or socio-economic status. Years ago, when she and her husband owned a Canada Dry Bottling Company, one of the

---

[3] Another version of this essay first appeared in *Saint Katherine Review*, Volume 1, Number 2 (2012). Reprinted by permission of the author.

teenage boys they "took in" to work at the plant was Elvis Presley. They thought he needed a break.

She took *us* in—the women of Saint John Orthodox Church. Most of us are converts to her native Greek Orthodox religion. She opened her home for monthly gatherings, where we learned more about our adopted faith, and she hosted a monthly book club, right up until two weeks before her death. She taught us how to make lamb soup for Easter and *kolliva* (boiled wheat) for memorial services. She oversaw the decoration of the funeral bier with fresh flowers and greenery for Holy Friday. And now she was dying.

"Father Troy came and heard my confession and served me communion last week." Her speech is slow, her breathing labored. "My grandchildren and friends have all visited. I've said my goodbyes."

She closes the book she's been reading, *The Kite Runner*, before asking me to bring her a Vanilla Slim Fast with a straw. "It's my dessert," she says. Earlier, she had eaten a small portion of shrimp and pasta which her son had prepared while he was here.

Everyday actions take on larger significance when someone is near death. Will *The Kite Runner* be the last book she ever reads? Will her last earthly sustenance be something as mundane as a can of Slim Fast? When I help her into bed and kiss her goodnight, all my senses are tuned to the life force in her room, which seems mystically charged, as if angels are holding their breath.

She squeezes my hand and says, "I love you."

"I love you, too."

"Forgive me, I'm too weak to kneel or even stand in front of my icons to pray tonight." She adjusts the oxygen tubes as I pull the covers up over her frail body. "I'll have to pray in bed." Her voice fades, her eyes close, and her lips move silently for a minute, and then she's still. The prayer is working, along with the Darvocet.

As I turn to leave her room, tears fill my eyes. The nightlight casts a glimmer on the gold leaf of the halos on the icons. The oxygen pump makes a steady whoosh…whoosh. I lean over her bed in the semi-darkness, listening for the sound of her breathing. There it is, matching the rhythm of the machine breath for breath. I want to stay through the night, but I need to sleep in order to keep up my strength for the days ahead. Reluctantly, I drag myself away.

Pouring myself a glass of wine and preparing the coffee pot to turn on in the morning, I take a deep breath. This feels so familiar, this watching. I've been here before.

* * * * *

The first time was in 1998. Dad had been a marathon runner for over fifteen years; Boston, New York, all the big ones. He even completed a triathlon when he was in his 60s. Affectionately called "the Guru of Running" by the members of the Mississippi Track Club, he and my mother owned Bill Johnson's Phidippides Sports in Jackson from 1982 to1997. They closed the business just two weeks before Dad's surgery to remove a lung. Fourteen months later, Dad died at the age of sixty-eight.

I had moved in to help Mom a week before he died. What the three of us shared during that final week of my father's life was the best and worst that we can know in this life. We labored through the days and suffered through the nights finding the intimacy I had craved with my parents while growing up.

Their 49-year marriage changed noticeably under the stress of my father's impending death. With all the distractions removed—business, running, travel, social opportunities—they now faced the frustration and anger brought on by his illness. Then they forgave each other.

Mom and I were Dad's tag team. Just as she ran out of physical and emotional energy, I stepped in, and the pace stepped up. As his pain and anxiety level increased, higher doses of morphine were prescribed. Forty-eight hours before his death, he asked for more meds. I said if I gave him more he would no longer be able to communicate. He knew it was time. I witnessed my parents' last conversation before Dad began the final leg of his journey.

Dad awoke briefly from his coma-like sleep, smiled and made eye contact with Mom and me. He responded to our words by squeezing our hands and then he was gone. As we stood there holding his hands, I was struck by the complexity of our grief, infused with a peace that came from knowing we had done what we could. We had been *watching*.

* * * * *

I awake to the sounds of silence in the guest room at Urania's apartment and hurry to check her status, stopping only briefly in the kitchen to turn on the coffee pot. *Whoosh... whoosh...* the oxygen pump greets me. My heart skips a beat as I stop to watch for signs of life. Her tiny body rises and falls with her shallow breathing. She's still here. I exhale quietly.

Two cups of coffee later I hear her calling. She's awake and ready to dress and have breakfast. She's weaker today, and I suggest it might be time to call Hospice. Urania agrees, and we call her son who lives in town. An evaluation will be arranged. She discusses this as though scheduling an oil change for her car. After the nurse leaves, she naps. The ratio of sleeping to waking hours continues to shift as her body begins to pull away from this world.

During the afternoon, amidst a flurry of phone calls from Urania's sons, daughters, and daughters-in-law, she clings a little more tenaciously to her independence, putting up a strong front. It isn't denial. It's a mother's irrational but unselfish, last attempt at protecting her children from the pain of loss. Oh, she knows they are losing her, but she doesn't want to inconvenience them, to disrupt the busy, meaningful and productive lives they have carved out for themselves. Urania is a second-generation Greek immigrant, and her strength and beauty have given them what they need to become the successful people they are today. It's been her joy to watch them live out their adult years with such fullness. But the love she gave them is the same love that is now calling them home, to her death bed. Careers and other commitments would be worked around. It's their turn to watch.

Her being overshadows our weak efforts at comforting her. She comforts us. We are only watching.

* * * * *

In the morning she eats a few bites and has difficulty trying to swallow three large pills she takes from the daily dose container.

"What are those, anyway?" I ask.

"Calcium and vitamins."

We look at each other. How important are calcium and vitamins to someone whose blood can no longer produce platelets? Urania puts the pills in a napkin, folds it up, and hands it to me for disposal. I watch as she takes another step away from this temporal home.

Our pastor arrives. We chat about my upcoming trip to Greece. He shares stories of his visit there a few years ago. The book, *The Summer of My Greek Taverna*, is open on Urania's ottoman. While reading it during the days I've been with her, she giggled from time to time. "What's so funny? I've asked. "Some things you have to be Greek to understand," she says.

We're supposed to leave on the trip in nine days, but I'd rather be with her. It will break my heart to miss her funeral. But the trip was planned months ago, and involves others. As the Greeks say, "What can you do?" Urania says, "Light a candle for me at the church on Patmos. It's better to have you with me now than after I'm gone."

Holy Communion strengthens her soul even as her body weakens. Her afternoon nap is longer than yesterday's. And then, it's time for me to leave. Her son will be with her tonight, and others are coming to town the following day. I sit silently with her for a few minutes, watching her struggle to find the breath to express her feelings. Maybe words aren't necessary. Touch might be better. So I kneel on the floor in front of her chair and we embrace. "I'll call you tomorrow," I say.

Being with Urania during these days has felt like visiting a sacred place. My steps feel lighter, and my mind flows to happy memories of times spent with her over the time I've known her.

The next afternoon my thoughts return to her as sunset approaches, so I call. Wanting to hallow this conversation, I choose my final words carefully. "May God grant you a peaceful sleep."

"I love you, Susan."

"I love you, too."

I can hardly breathe when I hang up the phone and try to shift gears to prepare for my weekend plans, the plans Urania insisted I keep. I'm going on a fishing trip with my friend and her four kids. I'll think of Urania at sunset, and I'll still be watching.

* * * * *

I call Urania's house before leaving. Miss Betty, the sitter, answers the phone.

"How is she?" I ask.

"Not good," Betty says quietly.

"Is she up?"

"No. And she hasn't eaten anything since yesterday. She barely spoke this morning. The Hospice nurse will be here soon."

"Good. They'll be a great help now. Please tell her I called and I love her."

I ache to be with her, but I keep packing.

Driving from Memphis to Arkansas, I stop to call Father Troy. The sun is bright just before slipping behind the foothills, but amassing clouds are dark and threatening. "Did you see Urania today?" I ask, as my phone cackles with static.

"Yes. I spent about three hours with her."

A pang of envy strikes my heart. "How was she?"

"She slept a lot. Then the Hospice nurse gave her morphine, and I helped turn her and make her more comfortable. Mainly I sat with her." It's his turn to watch.

I weep as I picture my priest's tears of love and sadness mingling with his prayers for this woman who has been so important to him… to all of us whose lives she's touched, and changed.

Turning off the highway, I check in and reach the deck behind Jo Jo's Catfish Wharf for sunset on the river. It's pretty, but it can't compete with the view from Urania's balcony earlier in the week. So I soothe myself with hushpuppies, catfish, and chocolate cream pie. When my friend arrives, we settle into our rental house for the night. I'm asleep as soon as my head hits the pillow.

Father Troy calls early in the morning. When I hear my cell phone ringing, I know.

"She died this morning. Her son was with her."

"Today is my husband's birthday," I say in response. My words have nothing to do with Urania's death, but they are a way of marking the day.

At breakfast my friend sees the news on my face. I cry into her arms. We tell her children about Urania. They know about loss—their aunt died four weeks earlier. She was just fifty one. The family's grief mingles with mine, tempering our activities with a somber overlay. The day I share with my friend as we spend the time fishing and listening to local music is made fuller by remembering Urania's spirit of beauty and celebration.

It soothes me to think that she is probably watching *me* now.

Sisterhood, and the Aged Mothers

Rosa Smith

2004

Quiptrych

Going, Going, Gone

I turn my pockets inside out
I turn my backpack upside down
only crumbs fall out
I put my mind in fast reverse
and settle my guts with a fearful curse
HOLY SMOKES! I just lost fifty bucks
as I shopped at the One Stop
with my head detached

Groceries and brains in a plastic basket
I did not divine trouble in store for me

I peer out the life-size window and speak
to an old lady in waiting
Is it still raining, I repeat
How would I know, she squinted at me
Gripping her black pocketbook
I don't even know who I am
Trouble is about to rain down
The enigma soon shows its scary face
Life is a game of roulette

it clicked at me
if you lose one, try another
But you can't dodge your fate
You gotta take what you rate
as you push through the revolving door
and return to the war.

Miriam Leader (1919 – 2012)

* * * * *

"How is your mother doing?" In 2004 my eighty-seven year old mother-in-law has started to ask me this on her weekly phone call. I am the go-between. "Fine" I reply. My mother, Miriam, is only eighty five, and she really is "fine." She is living alone and traveling around the world playing violin with the Young at Heart Chorus. I think that my mother-in-law envies my mother's good health and activities. Aside from the premonitions in her poetry, the only evidence so far of my mother's aging is the increasing prominence of her dowager's hump and her shortened stature. My husband starts to call her the "incredible shrinking Micky." Sometimes she needs a little help with odd jobs. When we stop by to visit, she asks us to open or close the windows in her old-fashioned house where time has seemingly stood still. My sister and I take her to the dentist to have her last few teeth extracted, and we take her to have her cataracts done, but otherwise she still mows her own lawn with her vintage push mower and proudly shovels the snow off her corner sidewalk. There is always a fresh pot of multi-bean soup on the vintage gas stove.

My mother-in-law, on the other hand, has had to give up all of her favorite sports -- sailing, tennis and golf -- due to circulation and breathing problems. She keeps up a preppy appearance in her tailored Brooks Brothers shirts and tan slacks, but we all know she has been diagnosed with mouth cancer and is desperately searching for a cure, missing my daughter's college graduation to fly to England for an experimental treatment. In absentia, she has graciously treated everybody to a special pre-graduation dinner at the Hotel Northampton. As we rush to get there on the night of the event, my mother runs with us, her home-made, vintage, gathered-at-the-waist, best skirt falling down to her knees in the process, all of us shrieking with laughter as we help her pull it up! My mother and my mother-in-law are each curious about their counterpart's lifestyles and wellbeing but don't connect directly with each other. My mother likes to hang out with younger people. Perhaps she doesn't want to accept her age.

2006

I meet weekly for supervision with my boss, Sally, a social worker my own age. During our meetings she often talks about her mother, who is living alone and showing increasing signs of dementia. Her keys and her car have had to be taken away after a series of accidents. Then she is diagnosed with cancer and goes on Hospice care. Sally frequently flies to Florida to check on things and handle her mother's affairs. When her mother dies, I consider myself lucky to have a mother who is still basically "fine."

2007

Mom starts having trouble packing for her tours with the chorus. She throws a few random things into her suitcase and forgets to put in basics like underwear and denture paste. I get an SOS call from the chorus director. I decide to go on tour with her so she can keep performing. Sally, thank goodness, understands perfectly and, we arrange for times off so I can travel with Mom to Switzerland, the Netherlands, and France. It is exciting and grueling, and when I get frustrated on tour, which happens several times a day, I try not to show it. My mother is walking so slowly we sometimes have to wheel her around, and she tends to isolate even within the group of aged musicians. I find this incredibly annoying and frantically chat up the other chorus members, making friends, as if to compensate for my mother's grumpy solitude. Another year goes by. Meanwhile, my mother-in-law has died before knowing about the changes my mother is undergoing.

2008

My mother trips on the corner of a table and breaks her arm as she rushes around her kitchen preparing for a show. It is her "bow" arm. I am on vacation in Tuscany when this happens, and my sister rushes to arrange emergency room treatment and re-hab. The arm heals, but my mother is never the same. She walks even slower, afraid of falling, stops going to rehearsals, and gives up playing the violin.

Even though she shows signs of needing more help, she sends the caregiver home and refuses to move out of her house. She instructs us to have "those people" stop sending her letters about openings in senior citizen apartments. My brother, sister, and I organize a family meeting that includes our mom, my sister-in-law (also a social worker), and my mother's eighty-year-old sister. Mom attends with pencil and pad in hand for note-taking. The upshot of our conference is that she doesn't want to move, and we don't think we can force her to, so we decide to find care for her at home.

2009

I begin to connect even more with friends about caretaking issues. There are long lunches with a hardworking co-worker who feels so guilty and indebted to her sister, who is the full-time caretaker for their mother, that she drives two hours every weekend to give her sister a break. My sister and I are talking on the phone more often. She lives in Vermont, I live in New York, and my mother resides between us. I am exhausted from balancing a fulltime job and three-hour drives from New York to Western Massachusetts every other week.

We are such a mobile nation now it is rare for multiple generations to live in the same house or neighborhood, so over the years we have adopted formal and informal group support networks which to some degree have replaced family ties. From consciousness raising groups, to group therapy and meditation, our insight and sensitivity have been heightened, although our actions do not always reflect this growth. Although I am trained to coordinate care, I find it is easier to make recommendations to others than to implement my own plans, so I spend countless hours hashing over our situation with my sister, other relatives, and friends. I try not to dwell on this subject with those who don't share my current challenges. It is a relief to speak with people who really understand.

None of us seem to be the "sandwich generation" charged with taking care of children and parents simultaneously. Mostly our parents don't live with us, although sometimes we have them move in, and occasionally we move in with them. As we consider the pros and cons of assisted living or nursing home placement for our parents, we also purchase longterm health insurance and apply for Medicare and Social Security benefits for ourselves, because in twenty or thirty years we, too, will be in our nineties. Most of our children are adults, hopefully independent, so we thought we were done with caretaking. Now we are mothering our mothers. The sisterhood continues.

2010

My best friend shares that her mother has dementia. A sibling takes her to live in Oregon. My friend tells me she feels like she has already said goodbye to her mother. I experience a sense of loss; the intensity of sharing the burden with my sister-friend has changed. My friend's life is no longer confined by her mother's needs. She plans a three month excursion to visit Buddhist meditation centers. I am jealous of her freedom.

I become new best friends with my cousin Eileen. We are both long distance caretakers, but Eileen lives in my mother's town, so we often meet for coffee to talk about our mothers. Her mother is ninety-four, and mine is almost ninety-two by then. Her mother's memory worsens, and when her usual caregiver gets sick, Eileen's mother needs a stronger support network. So Eileen moves her mother to a local nursing home, where she gets barely adequate care and doesn't know where she is, a blessing, because she never wanted to be in a "place like that." I am glad I don't have to visit my mother in a nursing home. At the same time I am becoming exhausted from the logistics of keeping her at home, which means hiring, supervising, and firing caregivers, scheduling her appointments, paying bills, and managing Mom's benefits.

When Eileen's mother dies, we hug and cry together. She assures me we will still have coffee sessions when I am in town. Will it be different now, I wonder? I am sad, envious, and happy at the same time. I'm glad my mother is still alive, but to be honest, part of me wishes the caretaking was over. I wonder how long I can survive it.

2011

Now my mother needs an entire team of helpers to take care of her. My thirty years of experience as a social worker has new and unexpected application. I have read about people who sacrifice everything, quit jobs, lost life savings, homes, and sometimes their sanity to take care personally of their parents at home. My mother did not want to go to a nursing home, and I had agreed to help her live out her life in her own home, but I am determined not to lose control of my own life. I feel squeezed for time, balancing work and visits to Mom, but I have also worked for many years and am ready to leave my fulltime job for a private practice. The pull of my mother's needs makes me believe I am ready. I bite the bullet and retire

Then the arthritis sets in. Mother can now only walk in the house with a walker. Increasingly she uses the commode or relies on Depends. Can it get any harder for all of us? Yes, we learn, it can. After getting stuck on the toilet and bruising her leg, she can no longer walk at all. I am reminded of the time she got stuck in the clawfoot bathtub before that. She switched to showers then, but a wheelchair shower now proves an ordeal. We experiment with a Hoyer Lift to move her, but she refuses that system, even though without it the will and strength of her home care workers is seriously taxed.

By August there are interminable talks with my sister. We have become daily confidantes. How will we survive our mother's aging, and how will our mother survive each new loss of her capacities? Our brother has made it clear that he is available in a medical emergency but not for management of care. Despite my experience as a social worker, I don't think I could do it without my sister and friends who are going through similar experiences. I make new friends, our aging mothers the common denominator. We learn from each other's experiences.

A friend invites me to a reading of Gail Sheehy's latest book, *Passages in Caregiving-Turning Chaos into Confidence*. We learn that as each caregiving phase ends, there is a "new normal," when your loved one's functioning or mental status and your own accommodation to it descends to a new level. Suddenly it seems normal when your mother can only walk with a walker, when she has to use the commode at night, when five hours of care a day are not enough. There are more "new normals" than we could have imagined.

Still, there are some remnants of Mom's old self. She loves her Klezmer music and visibly brightens when her family is near. In between bleating and grunting she laughs with us, although next thing you know she's screaming because she gets dizzy and doesn't want to be moved.

My sister and I have interviewed new helpers as necessary and have vetted live-in help. Waves of relief wash over me when my mother says, "They are taking very good care of me." She is having a love affair of sorts with the husband of one of her caretakers. At bedtime they sing songs at the top of their lungs and have meaningful talks about the after-life. Having meaningful relationships with her caretakers makes her need less from me.

So does having a wonderful doctor who makes home visits, a rabbi who comes to her house Friday mornings for a pre-Shabbat sing-a-long service, and a nurse who arrives monthly to cut her toenails. Two live-in helpers alternate overnight care, and several personal care attendants alternate daytime care. Between her rapidly diminishing financial resources and Mass Health, we manage to pay for all her needs and keep the household afloat. It is a worthwhile challenge.

2012

It is summer. My mother has lived in the same house for half her life -- forty-six years. At the end of a visit when I say goodbye, she doesn't want me to leave. Through my tears I think I hear her say, "Goodbye forever." We hug. I wonder if I will see her again. On the three-hour drive home I call to ask why she said "goodbye forever."

"I wanted to find out how it feels," she says.

Ode to a Momma
(Miriam Leader, 1919 - 2012)

At ninety-three the momma baby could not
get up alone and slept for hours and screamed
and hollered as if there were no tomorrow
when you moved her without permission.
You had to haul her out of bed and sit
her on the commode & wipe her bottom
applying barrier cream to her private parts
and then you smile 'cuz there she was delightedly
belting out her favorite Broadway tune!
Last night you saw her again in your dreams
witty with a touch of grump, eager to live
it up until the last possible moment,
young at heart but slowing down she travels
she dances & hikes & sings & walks around
the house alone and plays her fiddle, cooks
her soup of 3 kinds of beans adds a few veggies
and until her children take them away she heats
the house with the gas stove and trips on wires
from electric heaters she had installed
at various strategic points around the old
Victorian house.

Roar Above the Hum

Karen Clark

"This sucks."

I nod. "It sucks, *and* it sucks, and then it sucks some more."

Corine leans back and closes her eyes. The dialysis machines hum their white noise. Small, exhausted, indomitable. The puffiness beneath her eyes looks like crushed flower petals.

I look at her blood, flowing through the tubes, into the machine that takes out the toxins so she won't die right away. It seems wrong, having them take out all your blood, letting it leave your body and pass through a machine before they let you have it back where it belongs.

"Are you feeling sick?"

"Not yet."

"Good." I hope we will get through the three hours without one of those Cyclone rollercoaster blood pressure drops that leaves her nauseated, terrified, feeling like she's dying on the spot. She says she's getting used to them.

How do you get used to that? I knew I couldn't get used to it. I can tell by the way her fingers, crooked with arthritis at the top, tighten on mine as the tech slides the needles into the enormous green and purple bruise that provides the port into her upper arm that she isn't used to it, either. That she is afraid, every single time. Every three days, we have to do it, if she is going to stay alive. She calls the days she doesn't have to go to dialysis "my Hallelujah Days."

"Tomorrow's one of my Hallelujah Days," she'll say. "What are we going to do?"

"Well," I'll say, "there's a great costume show at the Metropolitan Museum. If you're up to walking around, that is. Or we could get matinee tickets – there are a few good things on the TDF discount site, but think about whether or not the subway stairs are going to be a problem. There's always the movies, and we can take the bus. Or we could just go to the diner and talk. What do you feel like doing?"

A lot of the time, it's the diner. The diner is the chain, linking days irregularly be-gemmed by an evening of free Motown at Lincoln Center, a trip to City Island for lobster (oh, how glad I am that we have a car and that my husband is a willing driver and event planner!) or any other gaudy, spectacular treat we can dream up to give her life zest and the motivation for dragging through three solid hours of hell, a day at a time.

I look at the digital clock on the machine. Two hours and twenty-seven minutes left before they unchain her. Unless her blood pressure crashes. Then everything comes to a halt until they get her stabilized. Extra time - long, agonizing minutes that don't count -and then the remorseless machine can pick up where it left off, draining out her blood and forcing it back.

I think about how much freedom means to her.

At our diner, she tells stories about her life as a civil rights activist in the sixties. She takes joy in relating her adventures from when she was still traveling the world – India, China, South Africa. She helped found a school in Africa, and they're naming one of the buildings after her. She shows me photographs – herself, smiling, shy and proud, as the foundation stones are being set into place. If she's in a confidential mood, I'll hear tales about some of the men she has loved - how in the end she never married any of them because she didn't want to be chained down. A lot of the men she describes sound pretty amazing. I think I'd have married at least one, if it had been me. But deep down, she has always been afraid of winding up with someone who'll turn out to be like her father – the abusive alcoholic who came home drunk, wanting to kill her the night she was born, because there were too many children already. "My mother had to hide me from him the night I was born," she tells me, grinding a bit of pepper onto her grits. "Can you imagine?

Ah, *querida* - " she spots the waitress – "*necessito un poco mas café, por favor. Gracias.*"

In the end, she won her freedom. She put herself through school. She earned scholarships. She became the principal of a failing Harlem school and turned it into a showpiece. She became a force in politics. When we go out, no matter what part of the city we're in, it's like being out with a rock star. People come up to us crying, "Miss Corine! Miss Corine! You probably don't remember me, but -" She always remembers them.

She sat by her father as he was dying, and she forgave him. She told me how she wiped away his tears. "Daddy," I said, "why are you crying? Are you in pain?" "No, baby daughter," he said. "It's just that tomorrow is Election Day, and this is the first time in 42 years that I won't be there to vote." The vote. The vote. They had gone through so much to get the vote. Nobody in her family takes that vote for granted. It is a sacred right; it confers a sacred obligation.

Corine opens her eyes. "Hey."

"Hey." I smile. "You doing okay?"

"Hanging in there." She shifts in her seat. My eyes follow the needles. I am always afraid an unlucky movement will pull at them and she'll be hurt. I can't stand it when she's hurt. But no. She settles more comfortably, and I let out my breath.

"Guess what?"

"What?" Her eyes sparkle. She loves surprises.

"I brought something." I reach into my bag. "Ta-da!"

"Ooo!" She regards the iPad with delight. "Show me how it works."

"Well, it's pretty neat. First I type in what I want to see, right here on the Search bar, and we can watch anything we want to watch. Music, old TV shows, all kinds of stuff. What do you want me to look for?"

She closes her eyes and frowns, thinking hard. A kid in a candy shop, she wants to make sure and pick the right thing. Her eyes open. She beams. "James Brown. Let's start with James Brown."

"Excellent!" I tap at the screen. "Which song do you want?"

She points a gnarled forefinger. "That."

I click. The familiar jungle-cat scream bursts into the air, drowning the hum of the machines.

Waaaaaaow! I feel good, I knew that I would now.

I feel good, I knew that I would now.

So good, so good, I got you....

Corine snaps her fingers, wiggles her shoulders, mouths the lyrics, does the classic seat-dance. I get up, do a two-step, spin around, and sing.

Waaaaaaow! I feel nice, like sugar and spice.

I feel nice, like sugar and spice.

So nice, so nice, I got you...

Other patients, after one incredulous look, begin clapping hands and singing along in rusty voices.

When I hold you in my arms

I know that I can do no wrong

And when I hold you in my arms

My love won't do you no harm...

A technician comes running over. "What are you doing? You can't do that in a dialysis unit! You're disturbing the other patients!" She waves an arm at the clapping, singing people tethered to their machines.

Our queen draws herself up on her throne and looks at her grandly. "Yeah? Let me tell you something. I can do anything I want. An-y-thing I *want*. I'm the client. You're the provider. That means I pay you, and you work for *me*."

A cheer goes up from the other patients, now her devoted subjects.

James Brown shrieks with rapture:

When I hold you in my arms
I know that I can't do no wrong!

Welcome to My Edifice

Nancy Clingan

Ruth's hand shakes while she holds her fork,
as if she's shaking a can of spray paint.
She's trying to eat. She smiles warmly,
and pauses to look at me.

Dr. H. says, "I've caught at least 500 babies,
somewhere around Tunbridge and Randolph.
One in a car, one in an ambulance.
That's all you do, really, is catch 'em."

Jane is wearing a Navajo turquoise ring,
on the same finger I wear mine.
We talk about it. She says her grandmother
gave it to her, "so it's really old, like me."
i ask her how old she is. She says, "105 in two weeks."

How does that feel, I wonder aloud.
"Well, I can't do anything about it.
Age, numbers don't matter.
I've seen children and babies fold."

In music appreciation they heard
Saint-Saens' Samson and Delilah
seduction scene . It made me cry
sitting in the garden room next to Suzanne.

Water aerobics are blissfully buoyant,
with a funny instructor skinny as a bean,
telling them to swim like mermaids.
They move their arms like Ferris wheels.

Someone reads poetry about Transcendentalists,
Emerson, Thoreau, Alcott, Hawthorne,
Mother Nature synonymous with church.
It keeps old minds sharp to think of forest cathedrals.

The men act like they're seventeen,
flirting with every woman they meet.
"Come sit on my lap, Honey," they say,
Lowering themselves into a chair in stained khaki pants.

"I am so glad you are here with me,"
Suzanne tells me.
"All I have to do is look at you,
and I know what to do."[4]

[4] Author note: I work in a nursing home. Suzanne has Alzheimer Disease. She is lost without me.

An Epilogue and Benediction [5]

Nancy Smiler Levinson

Unable now to engage in conversation,
you sit with me on a sofa, your arm tucked into mine
at informal Friday afternoon Shabbat services in Palm Village's
   lounge.

A young woman cantor distributes tiny battery-lit plastic candles
(fire regarded risky) and siddurs that you can no longer follow.
We share one; its prayers span our laps as our lives.

You usually doze off and on as those gathered sing and chant.
Yet one Friday I hear your voice, see your shy lips
barely moving, reciting the pillar of Judaism:
Sh'ma Yisrael Adonai Eloheinu Adonoi Echad...
Hear O Israel the Lord our God, the Lord is one...

With those few sacred words remembered and spoken,
I feel, for the moment, both comforted and exhilarated.
You, my husband and soul mate, have given me us again.
A pause for me to listen and hear that after a storm
a sound can always be heard—from a mountaintop,
a valley, an edge of the universe—
all-encompassing music of goodness and love.

And I hear the Hebrew words *zichronam li'v rachah,*
   May the memories of our loved ones forever be a blessing.
May we embrace all our blessings, as well as our burdens,
and carry them forward for our families to live
vibrantly, purposefully on life's enduring path.

[5] First appeared in *Poetica,* Spring 2003. Reprinted by permission of the author.

Contributors

T. M. Bradshaw has published numerous book reviews and feature articles in Catskill region newspapers and magazines. Her short story "The Cat's Jewels" appeared in the anthology *Crafty Cat Crimes*, (2000, Barnes and Noble Books). She is working on a book of biographies of local notables, *They All Lived Where!?*

Karen Clark received her M.F.A. at the City College of New York. She once owned a bookshop in New York and now edits, proofreads & "tries to make a living doing anything related to writing." She has been a contributing editor for two anthologies and has written a story collection, *The Grimoire Reaper* (2016.) She is at work on a novel.

Susan Cushman is the author of *Tangles and Plaques: A Mother and Daughter Face Alzheimers*, *A Second Blooming: Becoming the Women We are Meant To Be*, and *Cherry Bomb*, a novel, all published in 2017. Her essays have appeared in numerous anthologies and journals.

Nancy Clingan, an art therapist for 40 years, works as a caregiver, personal coach, and substance abuse counselor. She divides her time between Vermont and Mexico where she uses poetry and art in her life and work.

Sloane Dawson has a master's degree in art therapy. Her assemblage art appears in several New England galleries and private collections. With an interest in early aviation, she has published articles on antique aircraft in The Atlantic Flyer and The Pacific Flyer. At age 83 she is still a fulltime artist with goals and ambitions relating to her craft. She lives in southern Vermont.

Helen Dening has written for anthologies and devotional publications. Her teaching units and curricula have appeared in *Shining Stars Magazine, Bible Pathways,* and *Mailbox Magazine.* She now writes children's books and publishes a parenting column in her local newspaper.

Margaret Elysia Garcia is the author of *Sad Girls & Other Stories* and the audiobook *Mary of the Chance Encounters.* She also writes (and produces) plays, poetry, and essays. A reporter for *Feather River Publishing* and an editor for *Hip Mama Magazine,* she directs the national spoken word program *Listen to Your Mother.*

Tzivia Gover, is the author of *Joy in Every Moment,* and *Learning in Mrs. Towne's House.* She received her MFA in creative nonfiction from Columbia University. Her essays and articles have been published in *The Boston Globe, The New York Times,* and *Creative Nonfiction,* among numerous other periodicals, journals, and anthologies.

Kate Gray is the author of *Carry the Sky,* a novel about bullying without blinking. She has written three poetry collections and published essays. Her passion comes as a teacher, writing coach and volunteer facilitator of writing groups for women inmates and women veterans.

Elisa Jay recently moved to LA from Chicago, where she received a degree in English Literature. Her work has appeared in *Hippocampus Magazine, 100 word story, Word riot, Cha Literary,* *82 and *The Los Angeles Review.*

Caroline Johnson has published two poetry chapbooks and has been nominated for a Pushcart Prize and Best of the Net. A college advisor and English teacher near Chicago, she is at work on a full-length poetry manuscript about caregiving.

Susan Leader is a native Vermonter who lives on the homestead where she grew up. She is a potter who studied the craft in Japan and a poet who has been a member of the Londonderry Poets for over ten years. She holds a B.A. in art from Antioch College.

Nancy Smiler Levinson is the author of numerous books for young readers as well as MOMENTS OF DAWN: A Poetic Memoir of Love & Family, Affliction & Affirmation. Her poetry, fiction, and creative nonfiction have appeared in such publications as *Phantasmagoria, Confrontation, Poetica, Blood and Thunder, and Snapdragon: Journal of Art and Healing.*

McClaren Malcolm holds a combined degree in business, communications and economics from Yale and Minnesota Universities. She writes fiction, memoir, and interviews, some of which are award-winning. Curiosity along with a desire to serve combine to fuel her writings.

Deborah Marshall is an art therapist who works with grieving hospice families. She is a published writer and an award-winning photographer whose poems "are informed by life experiences." When not caring for her mother or grandchildren, she writes and creates visual art.

Ellen Meeropol is the author of three novels, *Kinship of Clover, On Hurricane Island* and *House Arrest.* A former nurse practitioner, Ellen's publications include *The Writer, Guernica, Bridges, The Cleaver, Dove Tales, Rumpus,* and *The Writers Chronicle.* She holds an MFA in fiction from the Stonecoast program at the University of Southern Maine.

Weam Namou is a journalist and the author of twelve books, most recently her highly acclaimed four-book memoir series, *Healing Wisdom for a Wounded World.* She received her bachelor's degree from Wayne State University and studied poetry in Prague. Her poetry and essays have been published internationally.

Sara Ohlin lives and writes in Bangor, Maine. Her essays have appeared in *Anderbo.com,* (as Sara Mitchell) *Trillium Literary Journal, Mothers Always Write* and the anthology, *Are We Feeling Better Yet? Women Speak About Health Care in America.*

Patti See has published stories, poems, and essays in *Salon Magazine, Women's Studies Quarterly, Journal of Developmental Education, The Wisconsin Academy Review, The Southwest Review, HipMama, Inside HigherEd,* and other magazines and anthologies. Her blog "Our Long Goodbye: One Family's Experiences with Alzheimer's" has been read in over 90 countries.

Rosa Smith has a degree in American Studies and an MSW from Simmons College. A clinical social worker, since 1980 she studied memoir at the Sarah Lawrence Writing Institute and poetry with Jason Koo and Lee Slonimsky among others. She lives in Yonkers, NY where she is working on a collection of poetry while maintaining a private psychotherapy practice.

Mary Wheeler has been an educator for 37 years. She has published two books for teachers: *Nurturing Writers* and *You Said Yes, a Supervisor's Guide to Volunteer Literacy Tutors.* Her published essays have appeared in several venues including *Lost Tower Publications, the R&W Journal* and *My Table.*

About the Editor

Elayne Clift, a Vermont Humanities Council Scholar, is an award-winning writer, journalist and workshop leader whose work appears in numerous publications internationally. A regular columnist for the *Keene Sentinel* and the *Brattleboro Commons*, a book reviewer for *The New York Journal of Books*, and a regular contributor to the India-based syndicate Women's Feature Service, her work has appeared in *The Boston Globe*, *The Washington Post*, *The Christian Science Monitor* and *The Chronicle of Higher Education*, among other publications. She published her first novel, *Hester's Daughters*, based on Nathaniel Hawthorne's *The Scarlet Letter*, in 2012. Her latest book of short stories, *Children of the Chalet*, won First Place/Fiction 2014 from Greyden Press and was published by Braughler Books in 2015. For more information, please visit www.elayne-clift.com.

CPSIA information can be obtained
at www.ICGtesting.com
Printed in the USA
FFOW05n0656210517
35854FF